party
gan

ADAM WARD

hamlyn

First published in Great Britain in 2004
by Hamlyn, a division of Octopus
Publishing Group Ltd
2–4 Heron Quays, London E14 4JP

Distributed in the United States and
Canada by Sterling Publishing Co., Inc.
387 Park Avenue South, New York, NY
10016–8810

ISBN 0 600 61080 2
EAN 978060061080

A CIP catalogue record for this book
is available from the British Library

Printed and bound in China
Designed by Grade Design Ltd, London

10 9 8 7 6 5 4 3 2

Disclaimer
The publisher cannot accept any legal
responsibility or liability for any injury
or accident resulting from playing these
games. This book in no way condones
alcohol abuse (underage drinking,
driving under the influence or binge
drinking). It is important that you
know your personal limitations and
when to stop.

Contents

It's your party!

Whether you want to break the ice, boost everyone's spirits or encourage a risqué and flirtatious game of confessions, here are 100 raucous and revealing games to help your party go with a bang.

From old favourites such as 'Bar Golf' and 'Fuzzy Duck' to confessional 'Naughty Numbers' and the ingenious 'Drinking Pentathlon', boozy party games are the ideal way to get your guests talking, banish inhibitions and find out your friends' innermost secrets.

How the book is organized
Divided into chapters to suit different kinds of party, there are numerous fun-filled games to suit any gathering.
* Break the Ice contains easy-to-play games aimed at making your guests feel relaxed, amused or plain silly!

* The Night Before the Morning After has games to give your party a lift and provide serious hard-core drinking opportunities.
* Games in Let's Get Physical require some planning, although the benefits of 'Kissing Roulette' will make sound organization more than worthwhile.
* Gather Round will ensure that a civilized dinner party descends into a hilarious night of debauchery.
* The Great Outdoors, with its chaotic games, provides wet-and-wild fun outside.
* 'Did I Say That?' has games to loosen the tongues and reveal the confessions of your nearest and dearest, ensuring that everyone wakes up the next day wondering what they said the night before.

Etiquette

There is a strict etiquette in drinking games, although this may deteriorate as the night progresses. Always drink from glasses rather than cans so you can check that no one is shirking their drinking responsibilities. People will be expected to pay a forfeit if they don't drink as much as they should, answer incorrectly or delay the game. As punishment, they can be made to do a dare, drink a measure of alcohol, or 'drink while they think', only stopping sipping when they have an answer.

Know your limits

Know when to stop, and try not to get so drunk that you find your evening is brought to an abrupt halt. It's wise not to drink straight spirits and good to set a reasonable drink measure such as one shot or finger's worth of beer at the outset of the game. Remember that all the games can be played for forfeits rather than drink penalties.

Using this book

Each game has detailed instructions on how to play, as well as a key so you can easily see how many people and what props you need, as well as the most suitable party to play the game at.

There is also a comprehensive list of forfeits at the back of the book, although you can always make up your own. Just remember, when composing forfeits, you, too, may lose the game!

So what are you waiting for?

Arrange a party and get ready to play these revealing, hilarious or simply intoxicating party games.

Break the ice

1

Whether you're throwing your first party or are having a group of friends over who've never met one another, these ice-breakers are just what you need to get your festivities off to the best of starts.

Choose it and lose it!

The perfect ice-breaker. No need for personal revelations or major embarrassment with this game, just a few suggestive laughs at the expense of absent partners and friends.

PROPS: PAPER, PENS
IDEAL FOR MIXED GATHERINGS
AND EARLY EVENING ENTERTAINMENT   ★★★★★★+

How to play

Hand each player a pen and a piece of paper and ask them to write down a piece of their property that they would like to get rid of. It could be a pair of trainers (the smelly kind), a computer, an embarrassing photo or a radio. They must then write down three reasons why they want to dispose of said item. For example, if the item was a radio they might write:

* 'because I can't turn it on'
* 'because it makes a dreadful crackle'
* 'because it's dirty'

Once everyone has finished writing, ask them to cross out the name of the unwanted item and replace it with the name of their boyfriend or girlfriend (flatmates, parents or bosses also work well).

No winners here, but lots of potential for laughs. The unfortunate thing about this game is that it only works once.

Hey, how's yours?

This is one of those games that can be played conservatively or raucously, depending on the mood. All it requires is a handful of adjectives and the power of suggestion to get the fun started.

PROPS: NONE
IDEAL FOR MIXED GATHERINGS
AND LATE-NIGHT FUN ★★★★★★+

How to play

Ask your guests to sit down in a circle on the floor and then send one player out of the room (usually the player to the left of the host). The evicted player becomes the 'guesser' and should remain out of earshot until the group call him back in.

The group must now decide on something that they all have in common: it could be a possession (for example, a particular CD, mobile phone or car), a physical characteristic (muscles, backside or fingernails) or a character trait (sense of humour, memory or libido). Once the group has decided what they have in common the guesser returns.

He must ask each player in turn, 'Hey, how's yours?'. Players must answer honestly but creatively and using just one word. So, for example, if the common quality is libido, they might answer: 'unfulfilled', 'immense', 'repressed' or 'fading'. When everybody's answer has been heard it's time for the guessing to begin. You can either give the guesser one shot or let him first ask the group three random questions that can only be answered yes or no before he starts guessing. Once the guesser has got the common theme, another person inherits the role of guesser. But if the guesser can't guess correctly even after being given extra clues, he has to perform a forfeit (see page 126).

Are you game?

This pre-party game will separate the party animals from the kitchen mopers! All the action takes place before the party, with the winner crowned at the start of the evening's festivities.

PROPS: SMALL PRIZE, CHECKLIST (WHICH MUST BE SENT OUT WITH PARTY INVITATIONS; SEE BOX) IDEAL FOR SINGLES' PARTIES AND PRE-WEDDING CELEBRATIONS

★★★★★+

How to play

This game is perfect for pre-wedding parties for the bride- and groom-to-be. It tests your guests' commitment to partying while also increasing anticipation for the events that are to follow. All you need to do is send out a checklist of the things each player must do the week before the party. They, in turn, must arrive on party night with evidence that they have succeeded in their trials. Mobile phones with integrated cameras should make this particularly easy.

The player with the most impressive haul of evidence wins a prize (free drinks all night if you're feeling generous).

Suggested checklist:

- Send an e-mail to an unknown person (from a mailing list or from the top of a message sent to you by a third party) asking for a date. *A print out of their response counts as evidence.*

- Buy a random person a drink in a bar. *Written testimony – a signed beer mat or receipt – or photograph will suffice here.*

- Have your photo taken (tourist style) with a policeman or firefighter. *You get extra points if this is in a fast-food restaurant.*

- Get the autographs (and ideally photographs) of as many barmaids/barmen as you can.

Who's got my banana?

This multipurpose game can be played for drinks, for forfeits or just for fun.

PROPS: A BANANA, MUSIC
IDEAL FOR EARLY EVENING
PARTIES AND BARBECUES

★★★★★+

Suggested banana forfeits:
* Eat the banana while singing a Justin Timberlake song
* Eat the banana and wash it down with an alcoholic drink (by the time the group has counted to ten)
* Peel and eat the banana using only one hand and your teeth

How to play
One player is chosen to be 'it' (as host you should volunteer to go first) and another acts as DJ. Sit the remainder of your guests in a circle. Players should sit close to one another with their knees up, feet on the floor and hands behind their backs.

One player is given a banana and when the DJ starts playing, the banana is passed around behind everyone's backs. You sit in the middle of the circle trying to work out exactly where the banana is. It can be moved forwards and backwards; and all the players must try to confuse you by bluffing that they have the banana.

When the music stops you have to guess who has the fruit. If you guess correctly you join the circle and the player in possession of the banana is 'it' for the next round. If you are wrong, you must take a forfeit (see box).

11

In six steps

The theory of six steps is something your grandma may have told you about... but this is definitely one game she won't have played.

PROPS: SCRAPS OF PAPER, PENS, A SMALL PRIZE
IDEAL FOR LATE-NIGHT GATHERINGS AND DRINKING PARTIES

★★★★★★+

How to play

Give each guest a pen and two scraps of paper. The players must write down the names of two famous people before passing the folded scraps of paper back to you. The names are all placed in a bag and mixed up.

The first player takes two scraps of paper from the bag and reads out the names. He must now try to link together a path of common acquaintances and events between the two as – according to the theory of six steps – it is possible to get from any one person in the world to any other in six steps. So, for example, if the names were Vinnie Jones and Lucy Liu, the six steps could work as follows:

1. Hardman Vinnie Jones starred in the film *Lock, Stock and Two Smoking Barrels.*
2. Guy Ritchie, who directed the film, is married to Madonna.
3. Madonna kissed Britney Spears at an MTV awards ceremony.
4. Britney's first love was Justin Timberlake.
5. Justin Timberlake has been linked romantically with Cameron Diaz.
6. Cameron Diaz starred with Lucy Liu in the *Charlie's Angels* movies.

You don't have to stick to a strict rule of acquaintance; in fact, the more spurious the connections the more amusing the game. Reward the player who comes up with the most impressive six steps with a small prize.

I'll name that...

Winning over party guests who are too shy or reluctant to join in with the fun is never easy, but this game might just be the one to get them in the swing of things.

PROPS: NONE ★★★+
IDEAL FOR WINNING OVER RELUCTANT
AND RETICENT PARTYGOERS

How to play

The party host – that's you – picks a category (see box) and starts the game off. You can choose any subject on which you can form an A to Z list. So, for example, film stars, famous novels, animals, countries, the scope is endless. The turn then passes round the group in a clockwise direction.

So, if you had chosen animals as your category, you might start with 'alligator', which could be followed with 'baboon', 'crab', 'duck-billed platypus' and 'emu'... and so on.

A player who hesitates, makes a mistake (for example, saying 'koala' when the active letter was 'C') or who is unable to add to the list is 'out' and takes no further part in the game.

Keep playing further rounds until only one player is left or until you are ready to move on.

Suggested categories:
- Film names
- Film stars
- Famous novels
- Animals
- Criminals and girlfriends (if you can't name a criminal you are allowed to give the name of an ex-girlfriend or ex-boyfriend)
- Singers
- B-list celebrities
- Personal heroes
- Capital cities
- Comedians

Variation

Instead of a player dropping out of the game when he is stumped (especially if there aren't many of you), you could always introduce forfeits to spice things up.

Animal magic

What better way to find out more about your guests than to listen to them compare one another with animals.

PROPS: A LIST OF TEN QUESTIONS, ★★★★★+
PENS
IDEAL FOR LATE-NIGHT GATHERINGS
AND DRINKING PARTIES

How to play

Gather everyone together and select one player to start the game. The chosen player steps forward and collects a list of written statements (see box). At the top of this list write the name of a player about whom the statements will apply. Choose somebody that is well known to the player and who won't be offended by the brutal character assassination that is sure to follow.

The first player takes the list into another room for 2 minutes and then returns to the room. The twist to the game is that each statement must be completed with the name of an animal. You, as party host, read out the statements to the group, who must then try to guess which guest is being described.

It's a good idea to organize it so that some players are asked to describe themselves, while others may be asked to describe someone

Suggested statements:
- As independent as a...
- As wise as a...
- Like a... in the bedroom
- As trustworthy as a...
- As beautiful as a...
- Tender as a...
- As fragrant as a...
- Shops like a...
- Dances like a...

who has already been the subject of another player's statements.

Variation

You can also play this game as a 'Mr and Mrs' version. Pick two players who are connected in some way (flat mates or lovers are best) and let them write down their answers about each other simultaneously. The papers are passed to a spokesperson who reads out the different answers. It's the perfect way to challenge your friends' undoubtedly distorted self-image.

Red herring

The perfect game to rid your guests of any early evening inhibitions and a sure-fire way to embarrass them.

> PROPS: A CONTROVERSIAL ITEM
> (PACKET OF CONDOMS OR EDIBLE
> KNICKERS), A DARK, NON-SEE-THROUGH BAG
> IDEAL FOR A GATHERING OF GOOD FRIENDS
> OR A SINGLES' PARTY
>
> ★★★★+

How to play

Ask each guest to put two small personal items into a bag; door keys, mobile phones and money are not acceptable. The items must be placed in the bag discreetly so that no other player sees what they are. Once all the players have put their things in the bag, mix them around and add in a potentially embarrassing item or two of your own (condoms, edible knickers, massage parlour card from a phone box or a miniature bottle of whisky are ideal).

Take an item out of the bag and ask one member of the group to identify who it belongs to. She keeps guessing until she finds the owner. Start with something fairly tame (perhaps a handkerchief or a lipstick) and gradually move on to more personal items (assuming by now your guests have got into the spirit of the game).

When you are about halfway round the group take out the first red herring and watch everybody squirm as the player tries to work out who the condoms or calling card might belong to. When the selected player denies knowledge of the embarrassing item, you'll have to keep the game moving without revealing that you put the red herring in the bag. Keep playing to the end of the group and try to pack in at least one more red herring on the way.

Big night out

This straightforward word association game can be played for laughs or, if you prefer, for drinks.

> **PROPS: NONE**
> **IDEAL FOR DINNER PARTIES OR AS AN ICE-BREAKER AT A HOUSE PARTY** ★★★★+

How to play

Players should sit in a circle on the floor or round a table. The premise of this game is that you are all going on a big night out and are discussing what you will take with you. Begin the game by deciding upon a word connection (see box) to link players' answers.

The game starts with the first player saying:

'I'm going on a big night out and I'm going to take my... (he must now name an item that fulfils the agreed criteria, in this case a two-word item) mobile phone'.

The next player must name another two-word item, stating:

'and I'm going to take my... brief case' (for example).

Nonsense answers are allowed providing they meet the agreed criteria of the game, so 'pregnant cow' would be just as acceptable as 'dancing shoes'.

Suggested word connections:

- Words that start with the last letter of the previous item (so, for example, if one player says 'mascara' the next could say 'antelope')
- Items of an agreed colour
- Words beginning with the same letter
- Personality traits

The game continues until everybody has named an item or dropped out of the game because they couldn't answer. You can now switch connections and play another round.

Variation

If you wish to play Big Night Out as a drinking game you can punish any player who errs, hesitates or gives an incorrect answer by making them take a drink penalty. Decide in advance what size of drink is appropriate – a shot glass of beer or two fingers' worth of drink, for example.

What if...?

This quick-fire but noisy game will lead to drunkenness and nonsense in equal measure.

PROPS: PAPER, PENS ★★★★★+
IDEAL FOR BREAKING THE ICE AT
HOUSE PARTIES AND SINGLES' EVENINGS

How to play

The players are each given a pen and a piece of paper. They now have 1 minute to write down an incomplete sentence that starts with the word 'If...'. Then the statements are passed to the game caller – that's you.

Shuffle the statements and pass the top one to the first player. He reads the sentence out loud and then has to complete it without pausing or erring.

The group now acts as judge and jury: if the sentence is funny or makes sense, the turn moves to the next person in the circle; but if the group howls and winces at an answer because it is weak or nonsensical then the offending player must peform a forfeit (see page 126) or, if you prefer, take a drink penalty. In the event of a dispute, the game caller's decision is final.

Suggested 'What ifs':
- If... my mum was Pamela Anderson... I wouldn't have given up breastfeeding
- If... I were propositioned by a transsexual one-man band...
- If... the whole world learned to sing in perfect harmony...
- If... the Loveboat really existed...
- If... I'd been in the Sex Pistols...
- If... I was the Pope...
- If... I was on *Pop Idol*...

You then choose another statement and pass it to the next player and continue round the room until everyone has had a go.

Guess who?

Guess the names of friends, neighbours, ex-lovers and other acquaintances using verbal clues, sculptures or drawings.

> PROPS: PAPER, PENS, PLAYDOUGH (OPTIONAL)
> IDEAL FOR DINNER PARTIES
> ★★★★★+

What to do beforehand

In preparation for the game you must draw up a list of subjects for your players to portray. You can either write out cards or, if you want to make things a little more interactive, you can get the players to each write down the names of ten people on separate slips of paper. The traditional way to play this game is to use celebrity figures as the subjects but for a more irreverent game you can use common acquaintances (ex-boyfriends or ex-girlfriends of party guests can be interesting).

How to play

Once you've got your subject cards together, shuffle them and divide them into two equal piles. Divide the players into two teams and give one pile of cards to each. One player from each team is appointed to describe the subject on the card (or let the job of describer rotate round the team with each new card) to the rest of the team. Each team has 2 minutes to guess as many names as they can.

The describer gives clues about the person on the card but cannot mention that person's name (if she does so she loses a point).

She continues to give clues until the others either give up or pass.

So, for example, if the name on the card was Darth Vader the clues might go:

* light-sabre wielding
* from the Dark Side
* father of Luke
* loves black capes

At the end of the game the scores are totted up and the winners either splash about in a pool of self-satisfied smugness or, if you're that way inclined, they impose a group forfeit upon the losers.

Variations

Instead of verbal descriptions, you could get players to portray their subjects through drawings or playdough sculptures.

What's in the sock?

What better way to warm-up the proceedings at a festive soirée than to get your guests groping around squeezing the contents of your Christmas stocking?

PROPS: RANDOM ITEMS, SOCKS, PENS, PAPER
IDEAL FOR CHRISTMAS PARTIES AND OTHER FESTIVE OCCASIONS

What to do beforehand

Fill a pair of thick boot socks with a miscellany of personal and household items (see suggestions in box) and tie them at the top. Each sock must contain the same number of items as the other; make sure that no items are visible through the sock.

How to play

Divide the players into two teams and give each of them a sock. On your command the players start to feel the sock in an effort to identify the items inside. They can either pass the sock around or huddle together and squeeze it all at the same time.

Suggested items:
  Any phallic shaped item
  A ring (curtain rings work just as well as jewellery)
  An unwrapped condom
  A gel eye-mask (the sort that goes in the fridge)
  A garlic press
  Vacuum cleaner attachments
  A star fruit
  Soggy toilet roll in a sealed plastic bag

The players have 1 minute to identify as many items as they can (and write their answers down); specific answers earn an extra point over generic answers. So, for example, a star fruit would score two points while simply a fruit would merit only one point. The team with the most points wins.

Party amnesia

You may have to work on your guests a little to get them into the swing of this game, but if you can persuade them that the theme for your party is amnesia they'll soon forget their cares.

PROPS: PAPER, PENS, A PRIZE ★★★★★★★+
IDEAL FOR SINGLES' PARTIES
AND OTHER MIXED GATHERINGS

What to do beforehand

When you send out the invitations to your party guests add a note explaining that every player must come to the party incorporating something into their attire that indicates forgetfulness (see box).

How to play

Give each guest a pen and a piece of paper as they arrive and ask them to write down the forgetful feature of the other guests' appearance. When everybody has had a chance to get a look at the other revellers, call the players together and get them to hand you their papers. Read out the answers to the group and award a prize (a bottle of gin is ideal) to the most observant player.

Suggested amnesiac features:

- Odd shoes
- Buttons out of sync
- Trouser zip undone
- Jacket but no shirt; bra and jacket but no blouse
- Hair in rollers
- Odd socks
- Pyjama bottoms and suit jacket
- Slippers instead of shoes
- Boxer shorts worn over trousers (Superman style)
- One trainer, one kitten-heel shoe
- Half-shaved face
- One earring

Of course, some players are bound to have forgotten to affect amnesia in their attire, but this won't stop others from perceiving some aspect of their appearance as obviously erroneous. Sensitive souls beware.

Checking out the competition

Breaking the ice with members of the opposite sex is not always easy. Thankfully, help is at hand in the shape of a game that will give you the opportunity to show off your powers of observation while enabling you to fill in the gaps in your knowledge about your fellow partygoers.

> PROPS: SHEETS OF PAPER CONTAINING TEN QUESTIONS [SEE BOX], PENS, A PRIZE IDEAL FOR SINGLES' PARTIES
>
> ★★★★★+

How to play

The host pairs up the players in mixed couples. Each player is given a sheet of questions to answer about their partner and a pen. The two players stand back-to-back and write down their answers beside each question. Once completed, they turn round, swap papers and mark each other's answers. Points are awarded for correct answers. The winning couple, with the highest score, wins a prize.

The questions are:
- What colour is their hair?
- How did they get here tonight?
- Are they wearing any rings?
- What colour are their eyes?
- What do they do for a living/study?
- Do they smoke?
- What are they drinking?
- What sort of footwear are they wearing?
- Do they have any siblings?
- What colour top are they wearing?

Super bowl semantics

This game starts quietly, but it won't be long before you are in fits of laughter as a friend tries to mime 'colonic' to you.

PROPS: TWO BOWLS, STRIPS OF PAPER, PENS
IDEAL FOR DINNER PARTIES
★★★★★★★★★+

How to play

Divide your guests into two teams, giving each player a pen and ten strips of paper (you'll need at least 50 strips per team). Every team member has to write one word on each strip, fold it in half and place it into the opposing team's bowl until all strips are written on.

The game begins when a player from Team A takes a strip of paper from the team's bowl and describes the word for her teammates to guess, without using that word.

So, for example, if the word is 'bra', the player might say: 'worn by women... Covers the breasts... Similar to bikini tops...'

Each team has a time limit (usually 2 minutes) to guess as many words as possible. Team B then has its go before the game moves onto the second round in which the players can only use one word to describe what is written. For example, if the word is 'bull', the player might say 'horns'.

Two points are awarded if the team guesses the word correctly. Alternatively, they can pass or ask for two extra words. If they guess correctly this time they are awarded just one point.

In the third and final round, the player has to describe the word through physical action rather than through verbal clues. For example, if the word is 'Arnie', the player might ape the action-hero-style of Arnold Schwarzenegger.

Dental delight

Simplicity is the key when it comes to word games, so forget all those fancy games that involve increasingly complicated and nonsensical phrases and instead name some fruit and vegetables while hiding your teeth. Perfect!

PROPS: NONE
IDEAL FOR BREAKING THE ICE
AT HOUSE PARTIES AND AS A BAR-BASED
DRINKING GAME ★★★★★+

How to play

In time-honoured fashion arrange your party guests so that they are sitting in a circle. The first player starts by naming a fruit or a vegetable (you can allow both or specify one or the other). The twist to this game, though, is that the word uttered must not be repeated by the other players and the player whose turn it is must not show their teeth (at all) when speaking.

The turn rotates round the group in a clockwise direction. But if a player laughs, hesitates, repeats an item already named by another player or shows their teeth they lose and sit out.

Suggested categories:
- Fruit and vegetables
- Items you might take into the bedroom
- Types of Indian curry
- Alcoholic drinks
- Parts of the body
- Insults (single words and phrases)

The game can be played either with forfeits (see page 126) or until only one player is left. If you are playing it in a bar, drink penalties could be imposed. It can also be played with any number of different categories rather than fruit and veg (see box).

Follow the leader

This simple game can be played alongside other games and will test your guests' powers of observation. See how it changes as the evening progresses.

PROPS: A BELL, CLAXON, DRUM OR OTHER INSTRUMENT TO MAKE A NOTICEABLE NOISE
IDEAL FOR HOUSE PARTIES AND GATHERINGS IN BARS
★★★★★+

How to play

Explain to your guests that tonight they have to keep a keen eye on you as in half an hour or so you'll ring a bell or sound a claxon (whichever you choose). When they hear the noise everyone has to ensure their drink is in their left hand. The next time the warning bell sounds, they have to switch their drink to their right hand, and change hands everytime the bell rings.

Let the other players know that you'll be watching them closely and anyone caught drinking with the wrong hand will be penalized – with a forfeit (see page 126) or a drinking penalty.

To give yourself a bit of a rest, you can promote the loser to the role of game 'leader' for the next round. This time, they are the person to ring the bell.

You could vary the proceedings by making the activity harder as the evening goes on – for example, when the warning bell sounds guests should hold their drinks in their left hand while standing on their right foot, and vice versa at the next bell.

The night before the morning after

2

If you're feeling in the mood for some drunken and debauched antics, then drinking games are the answer. They're also perfect medicine for a flagging party, to lift everyone's spirits and induce lots of laughs along the way.

The barfly's A to Z

Barflies and alcohol connoisseurs won't be able to resist this game that tests their knowledge of intoxicating beverages and offers the added bonus of a little competitive drinking.

PROPS: DRINKS, A SHEET WITH
ALCOHOLIC ALPHABET
TO HELP PLAYERS (OPTIONAL)
IDEAL FOR PARTIES AT HOME OR IN A BAR

★★★★★+

How to play

Sit the players in a circle. Start the game off by naming an alcoholic drink that begins with the letter 'A', the player to your left must then name a drink beginning with 'B', and so on. The game continues in this way right through to the end of the alphabet.

Players cannot pause or mutter and must say the first drink that comes into their head. If a player is wrong or hesitates, he must take a drink.

It's not as easy as you might think, but just to prove it is possible a complete alcoholic alphabet is provided (see box). (If you find the game too difficult you can let the players have a quick look at the list beforehand.)

Alcoholic alphabet:

- Absinthe
- Beer
- Champagne
- Drambuie
- Eggnog
- Frascati
- Guinness
- Harvey Wallbanger (vodka-based cocktail)
- Irish coffee
- Jamaican rum
- Kirsch
- Lager
- Margarita (tequila-based cocktail)
- Napoleon brandy
- Ouzo
- Port
- Quashbuckler (vodka-based cocktail)
- Rum
- Shandy
- Tequila
- Union Jack (gin-based cocktail)
- Vodka
- Wine
- Xango (rum-based cocktail)
- Yellowbird (vodka-based cocktail)
- Zombie (rum-based cocktail)

Crackers

Despite the crackers and wine, this irreverent drinking game has no connection with holy communion – though it may leave some of your fellow partygoers begging for divine salvation. Surely it's worth making a trip to the 24-hour store for a packet of crackers?

PROPS: PLAYING CARDS, DRY CRACKERS, DRINKS
★★★★★+
IDEAL FOR SPORTS CLUB SOCIAL EVENINGS

How to play

This knockout game intends to make the worst player drink the most; a familiar and reliably entertaining scenario. Remove a sequence of playing cards (from Ace to King) and give one card to each player. The number on the playing card corresponds to the order in which players will step forward to meet the challenge.

The player with the Ace takes on the player with the two in the first round. Each player is given three dry crackers and, upon your signal, their task is to be first to consume the biscuits and then whistle a verse of the national anthem. The first player to complete the task is the winner.

The loser takes a drink and faces a second round, this time against the player who drew card number three. If he loses it's another drink penalty and another round. The knockout format continues until the last match, by which point any serial loser will be in a state of drunken hysteria, rendering whistling impossible.

29

'But, honey, I love you!'

A simple drinking game that punishes laughter and rewards the straight-faced and disingenuous.

PROPS: DRINKS, CARDS ★★★★★★+
WITH STATEMENTS WRITTEN ON
THEM TO MAKE THE GAME RUN SMOOTHLY
IDEAL FOR CROWDED BARS AND SPORTS CLUBS

How to play

Organize the players in order of age and line them up. The first two players (the two oldest) sit down opposite one another across a table.

The players must look one another in the eye and, taking turns, must make the following earnest and heart-felt statements to one another.

Player 1 'Honey if you love me please smile?'

Player 2 explains that he cannot.

Player 2 'Now why don't you show me your cheeky smile, sexy?'

Player 1 explains that he cannot.

Player 1 'Why won't you smile at me darling... is there somebody else?'

Player 2 explains that he cannot.

Player 2 'If you don't smile at me, you'll drive me to drink... please darling?'

Player 1 'I would do anything for you, but I won't do that.'

The first player to smile loses the round; the punishment is to take a drink and then to face another head-to-head, this time against Player 3. This loser-stays-on format is likely to ensure that one player ends up suffering most, adding to the hilarity. If both players survive without laughing, smiling or smirking they both take a drink (for being smart arses) and step aside to let two new players in.

Cats' chorus

Take three tone-deaf friends, add alcohol, stand back and listen in awe to the dulcet tones of the instant crooners and divas you have created.

```
PROPS: SONG SHEETS          ★★★★★★+
CONTAINING THE LYRICS TO SIX
SONGS, DRINKS
IDEAL FOR LATE-NIGHT DRINKING PARTIES
```

How to play

Each round of this game is played by three players. You can either select the players at random or group them by age or drunkenness (it's always best to include a very drunk, loud person in each trio).

Each player takes a different song sheet from the face-up pile. The songs chosen should be well known so that players have a vague idea of the tune. Hymns, national anthems and TV theme tunes all work well.

On a given signal ('1, 2, 3' is the obvious one), the three players all begin singing their song at the same time. If a player pauses, loses her place or gets her words wrong she is 'out' and must take a drink penalty. The awful cacophony of drunken crooning continues until either all players have finished their songs (this is highly unlikely) or two have fallen by the wayside.

When everybody has had a turn, the victorious singers can have a 'sing-off' to find the champion of the Cats' Chorus.

Memory match

A simple game that will test the observational powers of your friends and punish those with goldfish-like memories.

PROPS: A WELL-STOCKED BAR, BLINDFOLD (OPTIONAL)
★★★★+
IDEAL FOR CROWDED BARS AND SOCIAL CLUBS

Suggested questions:

- Is the barmaid wearing a skirt or trousers?
- Is there a mirror behind the optics?
- Name three beers on sale?
- Do they sell Coca-cola or Pepsi?
- Do they sell Guinness?
- Name three bar snacks on sale?
- Are they still serving food?
- Are there beer mats on the bar?
- Do the bar staff all wear the same uniform?
- Is there an ice bucket on the bar?

How to play

Gather your players together and line-up some shots in readiness for the inevitable penalties. The game's premise is to test each player's powers of observation and memory recall. Each player is, in turn, either blindfolded or turned so that his back is to the bar's counter. The player is then asked two questions about the bar, any wrong answers are met with a hoot and punishable with a shot of alcohol. Questions are posed by you (the game organizer) but any other player can whisper a question to you at any time. The questions can concern any aspect of the bar or bar staff (see box).

House party variation

A similar memory game can also be played using a tray of spirits at a house party. Simply place a variety of bottles on a tray and let one player study the tray for 10 seconds, then ask him to turn away. While his gaze is averted, remove three bottles from the tray. The player can now look back upon the tray of drinks. He has 30 seconds to say which bottles have gone. If he identifies all the absentees he can pick the drink of his choice; if he fails, he must drink a specified measure from each of the bottles that have been removed from the tray.

Fuzzy duck

This game has two objectives: the first is to make your guests blurt out involuntary, childish but highly amusing spoonerisms; the second is to get everybody very drunk.

PROPS: DRINKS
IDEAL FOR LATE-NIGHT DRINKING
IN BARS AND HOUSE PARTIES
★★★★★★+

How to play

The players sit in a circle, either round a table or on the floor. You (as party host) start the play by saying 'fuzzy duck' to the person to your left, who continues the game with one of two responses: 'fuzzy duck' or 'does he?'.

If a player says 'fuzzy duck' the turn continues to move round in a clockwise direction; however, when somebody says 'does he?', the direction of the game switches and players must now say either 'ducky fuzz' or 'does he?'. Each time a player says 'does he?' the game swaps direction and the admissible answer changes (either from 'ducky fuzz' to 'fuzzy duck' or vice versa).

Anybody who inadvertently cusses, gets an answer wrong, pauses or hesitates must have a drink penalty. Have plenty of shot glasses lined up ready – there will be lots of mistakes and plenty of alcohol consumption.

The drinking pentathlon

Five childish contests, no overall scoring system but a rigorous code of conduct concerning the consumption of alcohol. The perfect event for those with impressive levels of embarrassment endurance.

> PROPS: OLIVES, STRAWS, COCKTAIL STICKS, MATCHSTICKS, BALLOONS, TWO BOWLS OF PUNCH, TWO TUMBLERS, TWO TEASPOONS, DRINKS ★★★★★+
> IDEAL FOR DRINKING PARTIES AT HOME OR IN BARS (WITH LIBERAL STAFF)

How to play

To win this alcoholic endurance event you have to reign champion in at least two of the five events.

Event 1
The 10 metres for olives

Clear a table and place a bar mat or similar item at either end to denote the start and finish lines. The first two players step up and are given an olive and a straw each. The olives are placed on the start line, the players get into position and on your command they blow their olives toward the finish line using the straw. The winner stays on; the loser takes a drink and a seat.

Event 2
The long jump

Clear a large area of floor space (make sure there's nothing nearby that could cause an injury) and set down five cocktail sticks end-to-end. One at a time the players try to jump over the sticks. The twist is that they must touch their toes in mid-air. If they fail to do so, fall over or step on any cocktail sticks they must take a drink penalty.

Event 3
Matchstick javelin

This is another head-to-head game, so two players are chosen to start the game. Each is given a matchstick and, from a line marked on the floor (with a bar

mat) they in turn try to throw their matchstick javelin-style as far as they can. The player who gets it furthest wins the round and takes on the next challenger. The loser takes a drink and sits out.

Event 4
Balloon sumo
Get the players into pairs and blow up some balloons (one for each pair). The players work together in this game rather than competing against one another. The first pair get into position, placing the balloon between their stomachs, and when they are both ready the group starts counting. The duo have a count of 15 to try

to burst the balloon using only their torsos. If they fail they must take a drink.

Event 5
The booze and spoon race
Assemble two bowls of punch, two teaspoons and two identical tumblers on a table and divide the players into pairs. The first two pairs come up to the table and when ready you call 'Start'. The players have 90 seconds to transfer as much punch as they can from bowl to tumbler using only the teaspoon. The player who decants most is the winner. The loser must drink all the punch in the winner's glass.

Couch potato drink-off

If you're too lazy to get off the sofa and simply want a vehicle to give you an amusing ride to drunksville, then this is the game for you.

PROPS: TV, DRINKS
IDEAL FOR GATHERINGS OF
LAZY SOULS

How to play

Check through the TV listings (or your video collection) and find a familiar programme that is strong on formula and big on cliché (soap operas are perfect). Alternatively, B-movies and music video channels can work equally well.

Agree on the programme you are to watch, and then agree upon a list of phrases or happenings that, when they crop up during the show, act as triggers for drinking. Also decide the measure of drink to take when the trigger event or phrase occurs.

Competitive play

If you have a mixed group with similar numbers of men and women, you can add a competitive element to the game. For this variant, music videos work best. Each time a male crotch is thrust during a video the men must drink

Suggested trigger events:

Someone makes some coffee

Close-up shots of cleavage

A shot of embarrassed semi-nakedness

Unfounded suggestions of homosexuality

Someone bursts through a door

A check shirt appears on screen

Someone's face is slapped

and each time there is a gratuitous shot of either a woman's breasts or backside (you decide which applies) the women drink. It's not clever, it's not sophisticated but drunken hilarity is guaranteed.

Bar golf

Pub crawls are innately competitive affairs (particularly when men are involved) but it is not always easy to assess who is the master of the Pro-Am drinking tour. Using a formal scoring system should go some way to preventing controversy... but, remember, if you cheat, you're only cheating yourself.

PROPS: PENS, PAPER TO USE AS SCORE CARDS
IDEAL FOR SPORTS CLUB SOCIALS, SINGLES' PARTIES

★★★★★+

How to play

Select nine bars that your party will visit on the night in question. Each player writes down the names of the drinking venues (these are the holes, to introduce the golfing analogy) on a 'score card'.

Players have a set time to consume a drink in each bar (beer is preferable, and 15 minutes is enough time for most competitive players). You, as party organizer, must also do the timing. When the allotted time is up, players put down their glasses and record how much they have drunk.

Suggested point awards:

+2 (double bogey)	= nothing consumed
+1 (bogey)	= less than half a pint consumed
0 (par)	= an unfinished drink (with more than half consumed)
-1 (birdie)	= one successfully finished pint
-2 (eagle)	= two successfully finished pints
-3 (albatross)	= three successfully finished pints

At the end of nine holes (that is, when you've visited all nine bars), add up the scores. The player with the lowest score is the winner – and probably the most drunk.

Cotton ball pick-up

It may sound simple but, boy, does it become compulsive. This game brings out the competitiveness in everyone and will punish the drunken and disoriented with yet more alcohol consumption.

> PROPS: COTTON WOOL BALLS, ★★★★★+
> FOUR BOWLS, LADLE OR SPOON,
> TWO BLINDFOLDS, DRINKS
> IDEAL FOR LATE-NIGHT HOUSE PARTIES
> AND AFTER-DINNER REVELRY

How to play

This game is best played as a quick-fire head-to-head drinking game, so pair off your players and clearly explain the rules to them. The object of the game is to transfer as many cotton wool balls as possible from one bowl to another, using a spoon, in 30 seconds. The player who moves most is the winner... the only hitch, is that the players are blindfolded, must keep their hands behind their backs and must hold the spoon in their mouths.

At the end of each round the balls are counted up and the difference in the two scores dictates how many penalty drinks the loser must take. So if Player 1 moved six balls and Player 2 moved four, Player 2 drinks two penalty units (you can dictate the strength of the penalty as you wish).

Your penalty units can be anything from a finger's width of beer to a whole pint!

To the happy couple

Wedding speeches can be tedious affairs; full of cliché and rhetoric. So, raise a glass to the masters of the banal and drink your way through the testimonials. Nobody will notice your antics... well, at least not until the dancing starts.

PROPS: PENS AND PAPER (OPTIONAL), WINE
IDEAL FOR WEDDINGS

★★★+

How to play

The game only works if you're seated on a table with a few like-minded souls who are willing to drink their way through the speeches and other formalities. If you get lucky and find a few kindred spirits, propose the game

Everybody takes a drink when:

- The word beautiful is mentioned in the same sentence as the bride's name
- Anybody pays thanks for 'support'
- The bride's father uses the words 'welcome' and 'family' in the same sentence
- Anybody mentions that you have to 'work at relationships'
- The best man refers to the groom's feeble capacity for alcohol
- Any mention is made of grandmother
- Any random hyperbole is used on the subject of catering or the florists
- Any mention is made of a deceased relative
- There is the merest mention of the bridesmaids
- There is mention of the weather

and get everybody to write down two phrases that are likely to crop up during the speeches. Agree upon the list, and then each time a speaker utters one of your soundbites, everybody must drink.

Lucky numbers

A competitive drinking game that encourages swift drinking and offers a simple and uncomplicated route to an evening of intoxicated amusement.

> **PROPS: DICE, DRINKS**
> **IDEAL FOR ROUND-THE-TABLE**
> **PARTIES IN BARS AND CLUBS**
> ★★★★+

How to play

The players sit round a table and in turn throw a pair of dice. If the total score of the two dice adds up to 7 or 11, or if the player rolls a double of any number, the roller selects another player to take a drink. However that's not the end of the story.

As soon as the selected drinker's hand touches her glass (half a pint of beer is a suitable penalty drink), the roller must gather up the dice and throw them again. If the roller is too eager, though, and goes for the dice before the victim has touched her glass, the penalty switches to the previously smug roller.

Presuming the roller's timing is good, she continues to roll the dice until either the drinker finishes her penalty beer or until another 7, 11 or double is rolled. If any of these combinations appear while the penalty drink is still being consumed, the drinker must take another beer. It is wise to set a maximum number of penalty drinks that can be taken during one turn (three to five is advisable) or the game won't last long.

Further penalties can be incorporated into the game, with loose shooting (when either dice falls off the table) punished by a drink. You can also make double-six a special case which triggers a group penalty (everybody drinks).

High tide

This quick-fire drinking game is an excellent way to ensure that any slow drinkers catch up with the rest of the group. So, deal the cards and target the shandy sippers for special punishment... you know they'll thank you later.

PROPS: PLAYING CARDS ★★★★★+
(ONE DECK FOR EVERY SIX
PLAYERS IN THE GAME), DRINKS
IDEAL FOR HOUSE PARTIES

How to play

For the sake of simplicity (it is never a good idea to make group drinking games overcomplicated) you act as dealer, game caller and umpire for this game. Seat the players and deal each of them four cards face up on to the table. Place the remaining cards on the table.

To start the game turn over the top card of the stack and place it face up on the table. Any players with a playing card of equal rank (irrespective of the suit) must drink, players with more than one card of the relevant rank must take additional drinks according to the number of matching cards they are holding.

When all penalties have been consumed, it's time for the next card to be turned over. This time the players must take two penalty drinks for each matching card they hold. The game continues in this fashion, with the penalties increasing in severity with the third (three drinks per card) and fourth (four drinks) rounds.

But after Round 4 the emphasis of the game shifts – the tide turns. A matched card is now a good thing, and the player holding it can impose a penalty drink on a chosen rival. And, just as in the first four rounds, the value of each matched card increases with each of the next four rounds, so, for example, a matched card in Round 8 gives the holder four penalty drinks to impose upon whom she chooses. Players can elect to give one player several drinks or can spread the punishment around.

Buzz

A classic drinking game that is more competitive and more entertaining if played as a 'battle of the sexes'. So, concentrate, stick to the pattern and watch your opponents drink themselves into a stupor.

PROPS: DRINKS – A TRAY OF PRE-POURED SHOTS WILL SPEED UP PLAY IDEAL FOR BAR ROOMS AND HOUSE PARTIES ★★★★★★+

How to play

The players sit in a circle and you (the party host) start off the game by calling out '1'. The turn moves around the circle in a clockwise direction and the next player must say '2' and so on, counting in sequence with each turn. All very straightforward, you're thinking; however, the twist is yet to come because there are certain numbers which must never be uttered.

In this game, players are not allowed to say:

* 7 and 11
* Any numbers containing 7 (for example, 27 or 37)
* Any multiples of 7 or 11 (for example, 21 or 33)

When a player is due to call out a forbidden number he must say 'buzz' instead.

A perfect run:

If nobody makes a mistake the first 17 rounds will run as follows:

Player 1 – says '1'
Player 2 – says '2'
Player 3 – says '3'
Player 4 – says '4'
Player 5 – says '5'
Player 6 – says '6'
Player 7 – says 'buzz'
Player 1 – says '8'
Player 2 – says '9'
Player 3 – says '10'
Player 4 – says 'buzz'
Player 5 – says '12'
Player 6 – says '13'
Player 7 – says 'buzz'
Player 1 – says '15'
Player 2 – says '16'
Player 3 – says 'buzz'

The game should be played quickly, with the count moving rapidly round the group and without hesitation. Any player who errs or pauses must take an individual drink penalty. But, when someone makes a mistake and gets their numbers and 'buzz's' mixed up everyone suffers. If a girl makes an error, then all the girls drink; when a boy messes up, all the boys down their drinks.

26,416

Super shaker

Even though this game of chance has few rules it does have the potential to intoxicate your guests very quickly.

PROPS: A DICE, A COIN, A CUP (TO USE AS SHAKER), DRINKS IDEAL FOR LATE-NIGHT DRINKING IN BARS AND AT HOUSE PARTIES

How to play

Like most dice-based drinking games, this game is best played around a table with the turn moving around the players in a clockwise direction. Agree on a punishment measure prior to starting the game, a small wine glass filled with beer is probably the maximum penalty unit you should use – unless, of course, you are eager to take the players to the brink of alcoholic oblivion.

The first player is handed the dice and coin, which are placed in the shaker. The player then calls heads or tails and shoots the contents of the shaker on to the table. If the heads-tails call is correct, she is safe and the turn moves to the next player. However, if she called the coin incorrectly, she must take one drink for every spot on the exposed face of the dice – that's bad luck if she threw a six.

Variation

If you want to intensify the action, you can reward a correct heads-tails call by letting the successful player impose penalty drinks in accordance with the score on the dice. So, if she calls heads correctly and rolls a four, she gets four drinks to distribute among the other opponents.

Sixes

Drinking games don't come much simpler than this dice-based classic. So what are you waiting for? Roll that dice, fill those glasses and drink until you can drink no more.

PROPS: SIX EMPTY GLASSES, ★★★★★★+
DRINKS, DICE
IDEAL FOR POST-DINNER-PARTY HIGH JINKS

How to play

Line up six glasses on the table, fill them with varying heights of alcoholic beverage and label them 1 to 6. Each glass represents a face on the dice.

The assembled players are seated at the table and take turns; the dice is passed round in a clockwise direction. The players roll the dice and pick up the glass that corresponds with the number thrown. If the relevant glass is empty the player fills it up; if it is full she must down its contents.

Fast track

To accelerate the action, you can use two dice, each working independently. If you throw a four and a six you must attend to glasses 4 and 6 individually, drinking both if they are full.

Pyramid escape

A simple card-based drinking game that can be played on an individual or a team basis.

PROPS: PLAYING CARDS, BEER, SHOT GLASSES
IDEAL FOR LATE-NIGHT DINNER PARTIES ★★★★★+

How to play

Deal out the cards in a pyramid layout, with five in the bottom row, four in the next, until the final single card is in position at the top of the pyramid. The objective is for players to plot a path from the bottom to the top of the pyramid, turning over one card from each row without uncovering a court card or an Ace. Should a player turn over such a card he must take a drink (see box).

Whenever a player uncovers a penalty card he must return to the bottom row and start again. The gaps in the layout are filled with fresh cards from the deck. Players must continue until they have plotted an unbroken path from the bottom to the top of the pyramid.

Suggested penalties:

- A Jack – one measure (this could be a shot glass full of beer)
- A Queen – two measures
- A King – three measures
- An Ace – four measures

Teamplay

It can take many attempts to escape from the pyramid, during which time the rest of the group can only be spectators. So, if you've got a large group or impatient guests, you can play the game in teams. The players all confer about which card to pick next (people will always have different opinions even though this is purely a game of chance) and the recriminations after any error are inevitably amusing. All players on the team drink when a penalty card is uncovered during their go.

Card suck relay

Admittedly this is not the most hygienic of games; those paranoid about germs should be excused. Thankfully, most of your guests will pucker up and rise to the challenge of moving a playing card around a circle using nothing more than suction power.

PROPS: PLAYING CARDS, DRINKS ★★★★★★+
IDEAL FOR HOUSE PARTIES AND
LATE-NIGHT DRINKING FUN IN CLUBS AND BARS

How to play

Sit your guests in a tight circle; each player must be within easy kissing distance of both their neighbours. Bring out a playing card and hold it up to your mouth, breathing in sharply to suck it on to your lips. With the card held by suction power alone, take your hands away and turn your head to face the player to your left. He must now try to suck the card from your mouth on to his lips. It's not easy but with a little practice it is certainly possible.

The card travels around the circle from one player to the next. But, each time it falls to the ground the group keeps count. If the card is dropped three times in succession the player or players responsible for the final error must do a forfeit (see page 126) or take a penalty drink.

Screen star

If you're an avid film buff, this game should hold no fears for you; if, however, you don't know your Sean Connery's from your Pierce Brosnan's you may want to sit this one out. Otherwise you may end up more than a little shaken and stirred.

PROPS: DRINKS ★★★★★+
IDEAL FOR STUDENT PARTIES
AND OTHER RAUCOUS OCCASIONS

How to play

As host you start the game by naming a film star; go for somebody well known as nobody will be impressed by your knowledge of independent arthouse thespians in this game. Harrison Ford, Brad Pitt, Ewan McGregor, Kate Winslet, Catherine Zeta Jones or Julia Roberts are the kind of household names that will make the game work best.

Moving clockwise around the group, the players must now, in turn, name a film in which the chosen actor or actress appeared. Each player has a maximum of 30 seconds to answer, if they fail to do so or if they give an incorrect answer they must take a drink.

But, the punishment does not end there. The group now has 1 minute to name as many films that the performer in question has starred in as they can. For each movie they think of, the player must take an additional one drink penalty.

Once the punishment is over, the game restarts with the next player in line selecting a new movie star.

Chopsticks

Who could resist a game involving nothing more challenging than fishing an ice cube out of a glass of warm beer?

PROPS: ICE CUBES,
WARM BEER, CHOPSTICKS
IDEAL FOR DRINKING FUN
AT POOL PARTIES AND BARBECUES

★★★★★★+

What to do beforehand

You will need plenty of warm beer, so empty the contents of some unrefrigerated bottles into some glasses and leave them to stand until the beer is suitably tepid.

How to play

Gather up your players and pair them off (men against women works well). The first pair come forward and each sit behind a warm glass of beer. The players are given a pair of chopsticks which must be held in their weaker hand. Their other hand is placed behind their back. When everybody is ready, drop an ice cube into each glass. The players now desperately try to fish the cube out of the glass using only their chopsticks. The player who removes the biggest cube from his drink is the winner.

The loser must down his glass of warm beer in one, while the winner is free to visit the fridge to find a refreshing cold one with which to celebrate his victory.

Snakes and bladdered

Take one familiar game – snakes and ladders – add a familiar aim (drunken revelry) and you have a guaranteed success without the need for convoluted explanations and rules.

> PROPS: A SNAKES AND LADDERS BOARD, COUNTERS, DICE, DRINKS ★★★★+
> IDEAL FOR DINNER PARTIES AND LATE-NIGHT GATHERINGS

How to play

OK, it's snakes and ladders with a twist in the tail. You play the game in the regular fashion but when a player lands on a snake or a ladder the game follows a different path, and one that invariably leads to alcohol-induced hysteria.

If a player lands on a ladder he dishes out the penalties; he counts the number of squares the ladder ascends (in a straight line) and then imposes a corresponding number of drinking penalties on the other players. So, for example, if the player's counter falls on a ladder, which elevates him three rows on the game board, he can call upon three players to take a drink penalty. If the ladder takes a player up more rows than there are players, everyone must take a drink penalty (no player can be made to take more than one drink).

The game continues until one player reaches the top of the board. But it's not the winning or losing that counts in this game, it's how you got there and how much you had to drink on the way.

Drinking at court

A quick-fire and uncomplicated card-based drinking game that is as compulsive as it is dangerous. Tanked up times are but a few card deals away.

PROPS: PLAYING CARDS, DRINKS
IDEAL FOR BARS AND HOUSE PARTIES ★★★★+

How to play

Separate out the 10s, Aces and court cards from a standard deck. The 20 chosen cards are shuffled and placed face down in the centre of the table. Each player is given a half-pint glass filled with beer and a full pint glass is placed alongside the deck of cards.

The first player turns over the top card of the deck and must carry out a task, depending on the card drawn.

* If it is an Ace – he does nothing (the turn simply moves to the next player); unless it is the fourth Ace, in which case, he must slug down the contents of the pint glass.
* If it is a King – the player can choose anybody else in the group to take a penalty drink (that is, down their half-pint of beer). When the chosen player has consumed the penalty the glass is refilled.
* If it is a Queen – the player must drink the contents of his own glass (which is duly replenished).
* If it is a Jack – all players drink.
* If it is a 10 – a word association game is triggered. The active player announces a common theme (basketball players, sexual positions, disgusting food, anything will do) and starts the wordplay. The first player to hesitate, laugh or mess up ends the sequence and takes a penalty drink.

Let's get physical

3

Ignore the boundaries of personal space and get up close and personal with your fellow party guests. Although these games require some pre-planning the resulting comedy will be well worth it.

Dressed to thrill

Take two exhibitionists, some inebriated DIY fashion designers, a few bin liners and some toilet paper, light the touch paper and stand well back.

PROPS: TOILET ROLLS, BIN LINERS, SAFETY PINS, TAPE IDEAL FOR SINGLES' PARTIES ★★★★★★+

How to play

Divide the group into two teams — boys against girls works best. Each team selects one player to be their model and have 5 minutes to give their chosen victim a makeover.

The boys are given two bin liners, some tape and safety pins; their task is to make an outfit for their human mannequin that vaguely resembles a wedding dress and optional veil (which is definitely worth the effort).

Using the toilet rolls, the girls must rework their model so that she resembles an Egyptian mummy. Depending on her modesty, bulky underclothes can be removed prior to the makeover. It's a fair bet that the boys will be keener than the girls to disrobe.

At the end of the game the party host must judge the outfits. There are no prizes in this game, but you could make the losing team's model wear the outfit for the remainder of the evening if you're feeling particularly evil.

Gloves on

OK, a props list that includes dice, an oven glove and sticky tape does sound a little dubious; don't worry, though, this game is about slapstick and nothing more sinister. Think of it as Laurel and Hardy meets pass the parcel.

PROPS: AN OVEN GLOVE, AN APRON, STICKY TAPE, SMALL GIFT, A DICE ★★★★+ IDEAL FOR SEASONAL PARTIES AND OTHER PRESENT-GIVING OCCASIONS

What to do beforehand

First, wrap a small gift (a CD, some chocolates or a bottled miniature is ideal) in newspaper or giftwrap. Use lots of layers and secure each with plenty of tape.

How to play

The players take it in turns to roll the dice, with the turn moving round the table or circle in a clockwise direction. When a player rolls a six she must immediately don the apron and glove and then attempt to unwrap the parcel. Meanwhile, the dice continues to pass round the group until either the present is revealed or another player rolls a six. If the latter scenario occurs the player who rolled the six takes charge of the kitchen-wear and gets stuck into the parcel.

More chaos

If you want to make the game a bit more chaotic you can prescribe that a player rolling a one also gets a turn in the glove. With this rule you'll get twice the number of player switches and double the opportunity for mayhem.

Take centre stage

Performance art meets Chinese Whispers is the best summati
for this entertaining game that is guaranteed to get your
guests mixing and your party moving.

PROPS: NONE
IDEAL FOR EARLY EVENING
ENTERTAINMENT

★★★★★★★★+

How to play

Select four people from the group and ask them to leave the room. The remainder of the party must now select a topic or an object that the group will have to mime to one another. When discussing the subject to be mimed the group must keep their voices low, otherwise they'll give the game away. As host, you can dictate the topic for the mime (see box for possible topics).

Once you've picked your topic, call in the first player. Tell him what he has to mime and call in the second outsider. Player 1 mimes to Player 2, and then sits down and invites in Player 3. The second player must now interpret the mime he has just watched and perform a similar routine to the third player, who, in turn, does likewise to Player 4.

Suggested topics:

* For the raucous – a sexual act with a particular type of person; for example, kissing an elderly person
* For mixed gatherings – drunken breakdancers
* For the bizarre – a dog skate-boarding
* For the malleable – tantric sex
* For space cadets – life inside a ping-pong ball

With each mime the story will probably become more confused. At the end of it all, Player 4 (the last to come in) must try to guess what it was his team-mates were trying to convey. If he gets it right, he can choose what the next team has to mime. If he doesn't, he has to perform a forfeit (see page 126).

Balloon squeeze

This physical game will lead to some bizarre and, at times, dangerous-looking dance moves. So, blow up those balloons, cue up a suitably upbeat tune and watch in awe as your guests make 'shapes' that will be worth recording on film for posterity.

PROPS: BALLOONS, MUSIC, NUMBERED CARDS
IDEAL FOR DANCING PARTIES

★★★★★★★★+

How to play

Divide the players into mixed couples and give each pair a balloon. You can play the game 'all in' or as a head-to-head dance-off in which one couple competes against another. Presuming that you opt for the latter, give every couple a numbered card at random.

The couples who hold cards numbered 1 and 2 step forward for the first round. When the music starts, each couple places their balloon between their shoulders and stands back-to-back with arms linked. The players must dance to the music while trying to turn around to face each other. Sounds simple enough, but the players must also move the balloon so that it ends up between their chests.

The first team to be dancing face-to-face with a balloon between them is the winner. If the balloon falls to the floor at any time, the players must return to the starting position. The winning team stays on and contests Round 2 against the couple who hold card number 3. The game continues in this 'winner stays on' format until the champions have been crowned.

Pass the orange

A physical game is, by definition, a sure-fire way to get your guests rolling around the floor in a state of hysteria. And this old chestnut does just that.

> **PROPS: TWO ORANGES** ★★★★★★★★+
> **IDEAL FOR SINGLES' PARTIES**
> **AND RAUCOUS GATHERINGS**

How to play

Divide the group into two mixed teams with equal numbers of boys and girls on each. The two teams stand in a line and the first player takes an orange and places it underneath her chin, squeezing it into her neck. She must now pass the orange on to Player 2, who must take it beneath his chin. Neither player is allowed to use their hands.

If the orange is dropped, both players involved in the changeover perform a forfeit (see page 126) and then try again. They continue until they are either successful or incapable of carrying on.

The orange (eventually) works its way down the line, and when it reaches the last player she must take it back to the front of the queue and pass it on to the player who started the game. Play keeps going until the first player has worked her way back to the front of the line.

Variations

If you don't have an orange, you can play the same game using the following:

* A credit card (passing it mouth to mouth)
* An ice-cream wafer (mouth to mouth)
* A balloon (under the chin if it is small and round, or between the legs if it's one of the long torpedo-style balloons)
* Cooked spaghetti (mouth to mouth)

Kissing roulette

After a few drinks and a little social interaction, what better way to end the evening than with some random kissing. Roll the dice and let the numbers choose you a target.

> **PROPS: TWO DICE, NUMBERED CARDS (ONE FOR EACH PLAYER) AND ADDITIONAL CARDS NUMBERED 1–6 AND LABELLED WITH A BODY PART (SEE BOX) IDEAL FOR SAUCY FUN AT LATE-NIGHT GATHERINGS**
>
> ★★★★★★+

Suggested body parts:
* The cheek
* The lips
* The inner thigh
* The navel
* The backside
* The nose

How to play

For all but the broadminded or curious, this game is best played in mixed groups. The host is game caller and does not take part in the debauched antics that are set to unfold. You do, however, divide the group into two teams of equal numbers. Deal out numbered cards to the players, which are then inspected and kept face down (nobody should know which number any other player holds).

The host takes the dice and starts the game (you will need two dice if you have more than six players on each team). You first select a girl at random and then throw the dice to select the boy she must kiss. Finally, you throw the dice a third time to determine where she must kiss him. Each of the six numbers on the dice correspond to a card that displays a particular body part, whatever it is, she has to kiss him there – it's in the rules.

At the next turn, the host chooses a boy first and then rolls the dice to choose a girl. The game carries on until everybody has had a turn at being 'kisser'.

Fancy pants

A riotous underwear-based game that is sure to have your guests rolling around with their knickers in the most almighty of twists.

PROPS: A BAG FULL OF
UNDERWEAR, MUSIC
IDEAL FOR HOUSE PARTIES AND
OTHER NON-PUBLIC GATHERINGS
★★★★★★+

What to do beforehand
Before the party, you must gather together a bag full of assorted underwear. Try to include a cross-section of garments but avoid going for the predictable. Grey boxer shorts and white briefs are fine but they can never match the comedy value of a leopard-skin thong or a pink PVC bra; so, try to find as many sexy items as you can. Garter belts, bikinis, camisole tops and posing pouches are all highly recommended.

How to play
Place all your items in a plastic bag and seat your guests in a circle. The game is played in the same format as pass the parcel, so cue up some music and when everybody's ready, start the underwear-filled bag on its path around the players. When the music stops the player holding the bag must take an item from within and place it on over his clothes.

The game continues until there is no more underwear left in the bag; at which point your guests will be sitting around looking like supermen doubles at a rocky horror picture show convention. If you feel the need to pronounce one player champion, you can count up the underwear and see who's wearing the most garments. Alternatively, you can judge the players on the artistic merit of their costumes. (Now would also be a good time for an impromptu photo session.)

The love statue

This physical game can lead to unexpected intimacy, embarrassment and a little contortionism too.

```
PROPS: NONE                    ★★★★★★+
IDEAL FOR MIXED GATHERINGS
AND HOUSE PARTIES
```

How to play

You will need two rooms and an equal number of men and women for this game. Take all the players into one room and line them up, alternating males and females. The first two players in the line should be a couple if possible (that way you ensure the game will get off to a good start).

Take the first two players into the next room and ask them to take the pose of a love statue (you know the kind of thing: limbs entwined, backs arched). When they are in position, call in the next player and explain that the two earlier players are standing in the pose of a love statue but that you think it could be improved. Tell the player she (let's presume it's a woman) can move two parts of the woman's body to enhance the statue and make it appear more amorous. When she's finished, tell her that she must now take the place of the woman in the statue, adopting an identical pose.

The next player comes in, the story is repeated and he then adjusts the man in the statue before taking his place. By the end of the game the statue is likely to be more about lust than love. This is definitely not a game for the easily embarrassed.

When the music stops

Adult variations on children's party classics offer the perfect start to an evening of raucous merry making, and what's more they require little explanation and no complicated props.

PROPS: CHAIRS, MUSIC ★★★★★★+
IDEAL FOR DRUNKEN HOUSE
PARTIES AND LATE-NIGHT GATHERINGS

How to play

Musical chairs is a fine game and should not be ignored by adults, no matter how debauched they are feeling. There are numerous variations on the classic 'stop the music, start the action' format. Two examples are outlined below and either can be used to get your party a little more physical.

Runners and riders

The boys are the runners and the girls are the riders. The game starts with one fewer runner than rider, so when the music stops the girls rush to leap on the backs of the boys, who halt obediently on all fours. After each round an additional runner is removed. You know the rest.

Lap-sitting musical chairs

The classic game with only a slight variation. In this version, the players dancing round the room are all of the same sex while the players sat on chairs are of the opposite sex. When the music stops all the girls or boys must find a partner's lap to sit on. The player who fails to find a friend is 'out'. In the subsequent rounds, one chair is removed each time.

The great belt wriggle

A simple physical game that may well lead to bumps, bruises, physical contortion and inevitable hilarity. The rules are few, strategy and skill are negligible but falling over is guaranteed with this bizarrely compelling game.

> PROPS: TWO LARGE BELTS, ★★★★★★+
> A SMALL PRIZE [OPTIONAL]
> IDEAL FOR OUTDOOR PARTIES
> OR ROOMS WITH LOTS OF SPACE

How to play

For this game you will need to organize your guests into teams of two. Mixed teams work best. Take two large belts and secure the buckles to create generous leather hoops. Place the belts at the feet of the two teams, who step into the hoops and must stand back-to-back.

On your signal the game starts and the players must try to wrestle the belts up and over their torsos without stepping outside of the hoops. The winning team is the first to get the belt over their heads. The losers should be made to take a forfeit (see page 126).

If you're feeling particularly vindictive, they can be made to contest the next bout of the game in a loser-stays-on style. You could also award a small prize to the final winning team.

Kiss race

A game based on kissing at a party? What could be more normal and what could be more fun?

```
PROPS: NONE                    ★★★★★★★★+
IDEAL FOR GARDEN PARTIES
AND ROOMS WITH PLENTY OF SPACE
```

How to play

Divide up the group by gender and put the boys on one side of the room and the girls on the other. Each player must give themselves a number, but you must not overhear which player has which number – otherwise the game will lose its important random factor.

As host, you stand in the middle of the room and call out two random numbers to select one player from each group. Presuming the host is male, the first number called out is for a girl, the second for a boy. The girl's task is to get to you and kiss you; the boy's objective is to kiss the girl before she has a chance to lay her lips on you.

Keep playing until either the game descends into amorous chaos or everybody has had a turn. The only prize in this game is the lustful embrace of your fellow partygoers. Pucker up – you know you want to.

Import-export

The simple task of passing random items up and down a hum
chain should not be too challenging, but add in some blindfo
and a competitive element, and it becomes more tricky.

```
PROPS: FOUR TRAYS,          ★★★★★★★★+
RANDOM ITEMS (SEE BOX),
BLINDFOLDS (OPTIONAL)
IDEAL FOR OUTDOOR PARTIES
AND ROOMS WITHOUT CARPETS
```

Suggested items:
* Rubber spiders and snakes
* A wet bar of soap
* A condom
* A peeled banana
* A walnut
* A ball of packing tape
* Ice cubes in a sealed bag
* Chopped liver in a bag
* A length of chain
  (with or without a plug on the end)

What to do beforehand
Assemble your items well in advance – you'll need two items per player, so that each player is continually moving on an item.

How to play
Divide your guests into two teams of equal number and sit them down in separate rows, blindfolded. The chairs should be arranged so that the players sit front to back.

Bring out the trays of items and put them to the right of the player at the front of each queue. An empty tray is set down to their left. On your signal the game commences. The leading player takes the first item from the tray with her right hand and passes it behind to the next player, who moves it on down the line. The first player now picks up the next item and passes it back. Each item is moved backward down the line until the tray is empty.

When an item reaches the last player in line, she passes it behind her back into her left hand and then on into the left hand of the player in front. The item then works its way forward until it reaches the first player, who places it on the empty tray. The first team to transfer all the items from one tray to the other is the winner.

The love train

A completely pointless and non-competitive game that will entertain both participants and spectators alike. Sit back and watch as your guests bump, grind and fall over on the chaos express.

**PROPS: NONE
IDEAL FOR LARGE ROOMS
AND GARDEN PARTIES** ★★★★★★★+

How to play

Select three guests, one man and two women or two men and a woman. The trio steps forward and you explain the rules. They are about to give an impression of a train and must listen carefully for your signals.

* One toot – the train moves forwards
* Two toots –- the train moves backwards
* Three toots – the train comes to an emergency stop

The players now take up their positions before the assembled spectators. The three stand one in front of the other with hands on each others' hips. The person at the front should be of the same sex as the player at the back, with the lone man or woman sandwiched in the middle.

To aid the train's rhythm you may like to put on some suitably inspiring music, but don't turn it up too loud otherwise your commands may go unheard and unheeded. Give one toot to start the train moving forwards around the room. The group should encourage the train to go more quickly and they should also ensure that the players remain close together.

With the train off and running you can have your fun. Sudden switches in direction will invariably lead to chaos, while emergency stops are likely to send the train crashing to the floor. Continue playing until everybody has had a turn on the train.

Pants

What could be funnier than putting on pants while blindfolded? Well, not much, apart, that is, from putting them on top of your clothes. Don't believe it? Give pants a go – it won't disappoint.

PROPS: LOTS OF UNDERWEAR, ★★★★★★+
TWO BLINDFOLDS
IDEAL FOR LATE-NIGHT PARTIES

How to play

Divide the group into pairs (mixed couples are best). One couple plays at a time while the remainder of the group sits back and admires the action.

The two active players are blindfolded and taken to the centre of the room (clear away any obstacles and items of valuable furniture). The duo are then given 2 minutes and a pile of pants, which they must try to put on over their clothes one by one. The players can help one another and take turns at putting on the pants. At the end of 2 minutes the blindfolds are removed and the underwear is counted. The couple who managed to put on the most pants wins.

Playing for drinks

Pants can be played as a drinking game too. All you need to do is appoint the group as a jury to decide if the pants put on are worn properly. A twisted gusset or an exposed label is punishable by the guilty pair taking a drink. And, to make the task a little harder, if they fail to reach a total of ten pairs of pants in their 2 minutes, they must take an additional alcoholic penalty.

Ankle racing

Running with your hands on your ankles doesn't sound too complicated – but wait until you try it for real. Few players will stay on their feet and none will be left with any dignity.

PROPS: NUMBERED SLIPS OF PAPER, START AND FINISH LINE, VARIOUS OBJECTS FOR YOUR 'RACECOURSE' IDEAL FOR OUTDOOR PARTIES AND LATE-NIGHT DRINKING SESSIONS ★★★★+

How to play

Count up your players and write numbers (one for each) on slips of paper. The numbered papers must run in unbroken sequence from 1 upwards. Shuffle the slips and give one to each player.

The players holding numbers 1 and 2 contest the first round of your ankle racing challenge. The two players step up to the start line and get in position, placing their hands on their ankles so that they are hunched over. Upon your command they race for the finish line. If they fall over they must go back to the start again.

It's also a great idea to build a mini 'racecourse' where your players have to pick up objects with their teeth and jump over mini hurdles as part of the race for the finish line.

The first player to cross the finishing line is the winner. The loser performs a forfeit (see page 126) and the winner stays on to contest Player 3.

The game continues until all players have had a turn. The winner of the last round is the champion and should be awarded an appropriate prize – a magnum of champagne shaken and consumed on an impromptu podium is a fitting reward.

The circle of truth

This physical game requires only minimal movement but it provides endless opportunity for intimacy and stark revelations about the private lives of your guests.

PROPS: STRONG CHAIRS, NUMBERED LABELS FOR CHAIRS IDEAL FOR HOUSE PARTIES AND OTHER MIXED GATHERINGS ★★★★★★+

How to play

Seat your players in a circle on strong chairs (which should be numbered so that everybody knows where they were seated at the start of play).

Start the game yourself by calling out a question, preferably one that is slightly risqué, which enquires about the others' past experiences. So, for example, you might ask: 'Who has dated two or more siblings from the same family?'.

Anybody who can answer 'yes' to the question must move one place to her right. If the chair is empty the player sits down as usual, but if it is occupied she must sit on the lap of the person already there. At certain points in the game there will be huge pile-ups of players on particular chairs.

Each player gets a chance to pose a question, as the turn passes round the group in a clockwise direction (according to the original seating plan).

The first player to make it back to her starting chair wins the game.

Squeal piggy squeal

It may be a children's classic but even today a game that requires your guests to sit on one another's laps and squeal like a pig should not be ignored. What could be more natural?

PROPS: A BLINDFOLD, A PILLOW
IDEAL FOR ANY MIXED GATHERING

How to play

Sit your guests in a circle and select one player (this can be done randomly or through numbered cards) to act as 'detective'. The player selected is given a pillow, blindfolded, spun round a few times (for the purposes of disorientation) and sat in the middle of the circle. The other players, meanwhile, swap places, so by the time the game begins the blindfolded detective has no idea who's sitting where.

The detective places the pillow on the lap of a randomly selected player, sits down and says 'squeal piggy squeal!'. The player must now give an impersonation of a pig – snorting, snuffling and squealing are all acceptable noises. When the impersonation is over, the detective tries to guess the identity of the pig impersonator.

If she guesses correctly, her turn comes to an end; but if she guesses incorrectly the group reshuffles and the detective must go through the whole scenario again. The game continues until each player has identified a pig impersonator.

Gather round

4

Some games just work best when the players are seated round a table and so make perfect additions to any modern dinner party. But even if you're not being 'the host with the most', then you can sit everyone in a circle and the games work just as well. So, give it a go.

Bubblegum sculpture

A game that tests not only your powers of mastication but al▶
your creative talents – who says chewing gum is bad for you?

PROPS: BUBBLEGUM, ★★★★★★★★+
TOOTHPICKS (OR COCKTAIL
STICKS) AND SUBJECT CARDS (OPTIONAL)
IDEAL FOR MIXED GATHERINGS AND DINNER PARTIES

Suggested subject cards:
* Animals
* Drunkenness
* Love
* Lust
* Violence
* Bruce Lee
* Darth Vader
* Ozzie Osbourne
* Jordan
* Barbra Streisand

How to play

You can play this game in several
ways (see below) but the basic
premise of the game is the same.
Players are given a packet of gum
and a toothpick and must chew
the gum until it is malleable. Then,
using only the toothpick, they
must sculpt a model to represent
the subject identified on the card
they have been given.

Head-to-head

Two players are given the same
subject to model and 90 seconds in
which to create their masterpiece.
The group sit in judgement and
determine who's model is best. The
loser can be made to face a forfeit
(see page 126).

Teamplay

Divide the players into two equal
groups (men against women, for
example). Players have 90 seconds
to depict the subject on the card.
The sculptor's team-mates then
try to guess what was on the card
in 1 minute. To make the game
slightly easier, you can allow
them to ask questions but the
sculptor can only answer yes or
no. If they guess correctly the
team is awarded a point. If they
get it wrong or cannot answer the
other team get a chance to steal
the point. When everybody has
had a turn the scores are totalled
up and the champions crowned.
The losers should of course be
made to take a group forfeit (see
page 126).

Acronyms

A silly word game that will make you giggle and get you thinking. It will also lull your friends into a false sense of security with its inoffensive but infectious gameplay.

PROPS: WORD LISTS (OPTIONAL)
IDEAL FOR DINNER PARTIES
AND MIXED GATHERINGS

How to play

As host of the party you have the honour of starting the game. Think of a four-letter word and point at another player, stating that word clearly. You can choose any word you like. Say, for example 'SEAT', and point at any player.

The appointed player must take the initial letter 'S' and say the first noun that he thinks of that starts with the letter. In our example, the player says 'Sarah'; he must then point to another player to continue the game.

Player 2 thinks of a verb beginning with the word's second letter; in our example it's 'E' and so the player says 'eats'. The game continues with the final two players saying the first words they think of that start with the relevant letter. In these rounds, verbs, nouns, adverbs and adjectives can all be used. To complete our scenario, the last two players go for the words 'albino' and 'tarantulas'.

So, our acronym SEAT becomes Sarah eats albino tarantulas. Doesn't sound too hysterical when you read it on a printed page, but stir in a dozen people and the high jinks of a social occasion and you'll soon see the funny side.

Who am I?

No complicated rules, props or space requirements here; just straightforward honest to goodness gameplay. This game is perfect for starting any party. Clever souls will revel in the game's deductive qualities while the rest amuse themselves at the nonsense uttered by everybody else.

PROPS: STICKY MEMO NOTES, PENS
IDEAL FOR MOVING FROM DINNER
TO PARTY MODE ★★★★+

Suggested categories:
* Reality TV 'stars'
* Tabloid celebs
* Pop Idol finalists
* Actors or actresses
* Cartoon characters
* Footballers (and their wives)

How to play

Each player is given a sticky memo note and a pen. The players write down the name of a famous person and then stick the paper to the forehead of the player on their left; it is, of course, imperative that they do not see the name.

Have a good look round the table and see who's who. There'll be a few chuckles and titters but try not to give any clues away. Now the questioning begins.

The host starts and you can ask the group a direct question about the person whose name is on your forehead. The question can only be met with a 'yes' or a 'no' answer. So, for example, you might ask 'Am I alive?' or 'Am I a man?'. You may continue to ask questions until either you are ready to guess the name or ask a question that is met with a 'no' answer. When this latter scenario occurs the turn moves to the player on your left.

The winner is the player who guesses her identity first. If you want to restrict the scope of the game you can insist that the names of the celebrities are chosen from particular categories (see box).

Wink murder

It may be a time-honoured classic but this game is no less compelling today than it was more than a century ago. Played in the right spirit, and maybe after a few drinks, the dying swan routines and the sense of tension will soon have your guests hooked.

> PROPS: PLAYING CARDS
> IDEAL FOR MIXED GATHERINGS ★★★★★+
> AND DINNER PARTIES

How to play

Remove as many cards from the deck as there are players in the game, making sure that one of them is the Ace of spades. Shuffle the cards and give one to each of the players.

Everybody looks at their cards and puts them aside. The player who gets the Ace of spades is the murderer. The game begins when the cards are put down.

The murderer must try to 'kill' the other players by winking at them, but she must try to do so without detection. Any player that sees he is winked at 'dies' (cue amateur dramatics and hysterical screaming). The murdered player is, as you might expect, out of the game.

The killer continues her mayhem until a player believes he knows the identity of the optically challenged assassin. At this point, the accuser invites the other players to close their eyes and put their right hands on the table. He then taps the hand of the player he suspects. If his suspicions are confirmed, the game is over, the murderer is caught and the celebrations commence. If he is wrong, he must leave the game.

Q & A with a twist

A quick-fire question-and-answer game that requires powers of concentration that will rapidly diminish as any drinking gets underway. Chaos, laughter and no little embarrassment will soon fill the void.

PROPS: A LIST OF QUESTIONS [SEE BOX] ★★★★★★+
IDEAL FOR EARLY EVENING ENTERTAINMENT

How to play

Each player has 1 minute to answer the questions without pausing, lying, mumbling or giving the wrong answer. If there is any contravention of the rules it is punishable with a forfeit (see page 126). To avoid any penalties, players must answer the questions in an 'out of sync' fashion, replying to each new question with the answer to the previous one (see example right).

The group act as judge and jury and will soon grumble if they think punishment is due.

Suggested questions and answers:

1 What's your name? (no answer)
2 Who's your favourite sex symbol?
   Player replies with his own name
3 Name somebody physically repulsive?
   Darryl Hannah
4 Who is the last person you told you loved?
   Barry in the fish-and-chip shop
5 Name somebody you've betrayed?
   My mum
6 Name something or somebody you're obsessed by?
   My ex-girlfriend Katie
7 Name something or somebody you've pretended to like?
   Football
8 What would you ban if you could?
   Poetry
9 Name someone you admire?
   Queue-jumping
10 Name a publicity-seeking celebrity?
   Mother Theresa
11 Who would you swap places with in the public eye?
   Britney Spears

Sculpt, mime or draw

A quirky game that will reward the skills of the artistic all-rounder or – as is more likely – amuse and confuse the watching gallery as they try to guess what each of the players is trying to represent.

PROPS: MODELLING CLAY, PAPER, CRAYONS, SUBJECT CARDS, DICE ★★★★★★+
IDEAL FOR DINNER PARTIES
AND OTHER MIXED GATHERINGS

Suggested subject cards:
* Motor vehicles
* True love
* Zoo animals
* Lust
* Ménage à trois
* Drunkenness

How to play

Clear a table and gather the group together. The first player steps forward and takes a subject card from the pile (see box). He looks at the card but does not tell the other players what it says. He must then roll the dice to determine the medium through which he will convey the subject to his audience.

* If he rolls a one or a two, he must use the power of mime.
* If he rolls a three or a four, he must draw an artwork using crayons and his weaker hand.
* If he rolls a five or a six, he must make a clay sculpture.

Each player has 2 minutes to flex their creative muscles. At the end of the allotted time the group must try to guess what the subject card said. If they cannot guess, you can allow them each to ask the artist one direct question, to which he must reply with either 'yes' or 'no'.

To add a little spice to the proceedings you can play boys against girls awarding the teams a point each time they guess the subject being portrayed by their representative artist. When everybody's taken a turn the scores are totted up and prizes or forfeits (see page 126) awarded.

Anecdotal charades

There's nothing quite like an irreverent remix on a classic game to inspire your guests to get into the swing of things.

> PROPS: NONE
> IDEAL FOR DRUNKEN TYPES
> AND CLOSE FRIENDS
> ★★★★★★★★+

How to play

Divide the group up into two teams; boys and girls is the obvious criteria, though you must have equal numbers in each team. The basic gameplay is the same as traditional charades: so, a player from each team takes it in turn to mime to the remainder of their team-mates. If the team guess the mime in 1 minute, they get a point; if not, the opposing team get a chance to guess.

So, where's the remix? Well, the twist is that the mimes must portray an anecdote or event that the players either have been party to or have witnessed. The anecdote could be about a drunken evening, some romantic skulduggery or some kind of deviant behaviour – it may even include all three. For example, a mime about the time that Kevin chatted up a drag queen would be ideal.

If you want to play the game in a vaguely controlled way you can play for points, totting up the scores once every player has had a turn. Alternatively, if chaos is more to your taste, you can play for forfeits (see page 126), making the whole team suffer a penalty if they are unable to guess a mime.

My filthy, beloved underwear

Ever wanted to make your friends say some silly things, well this game gives you that chance. It's a simple word game that will make everyone laugh and banish any inhibitions.

```
PROPS: NOUN CARDS           ★★★★★+
IDEAL FOR POST-DINNER PARTY
HILARITY
```

Suggested nouns:

* Underwear
* Libido
* Complexion
* Genitals
* Husband
* Mother
* Grandfather
* Breasts
* Dependency
* Psychosis

How to play

The aim of the game is for the group to complete five-word sentences that are as ludicrous as they are amusing. The players sit round a table or in a circle and the player to the left of the host starts the game by taking a noun card from the middle of the floor (see box). He looks at the card but doesn't tell anybody what it says. The next three players must each say an adjective in turn and then Player 1 completes the sentence with the noun from the card.

The sentence could work out as follows.

* Player 1 – 'My (the sentence always starts with 'My')
* Player 2 – 'beautiful' (adjective 1)
* Player 3 – 'beloved' (adjective 2)
* Player 4 – 'filthy' (adjective 3)
* Player 1 again – 'underwear' (noun)

The player who drew the noun card reads out the sentence and pulls an incredulous face.

Saucy stories

A simple story-telling game that – if guided correctly – should spawn some risqué, bizarre and hilarious tales.

PROPS: STRIPS OF PAPER, A PEN ★★★★★★+
IDEAL FOR LATE-NIGHT PARTIES
AND DRUNKEN EVENINGS WITH FRIENDS

Suggested random words:
* Gusset
* Achingly
* Intimidated
* Stimulated
* Terrified

Suggested random phrases:
* She was stunned by its size
* He was truly a master
* She had no towel

How to play

The first phase of this game is for the players to each think of a random word and phrase from a sentence (see box). The more outrageous or bizarre the words and phrases the more amusing the game. The host writes down each player's contribution on separate strips of paper or cards, folds them over and places them in two piles which should be shuffled and placed face down on the floor).

Players take a card from each pile, look at them and then put them to one side. You, as game organizer, start the play by telling the beginning of a story. Try to make your contribution suggestive and amusing.

So, for example 'Kylie woke up tingling, she was very excited but she had no idea where she was...'. You then hand over to the player on your left who must continue the story while also integrating the words and phrases on his cards into the tale. Each time a player incorporates a word or phrase he holds up the corresponding card.

You can play the game just for fun but if you want to add a competitive element you can introduce time limits and forfeits. Players are given 30 seconds to mention all the words on their cards. If they fail to do so, they perform a forfeit (see page 126). Quantum leaps, where players suddenly and without sufficient preamble introduce one of the words from their cards should be met with groaning and an additional penalty.

The name game

A noisy game that is easily explained but that becomes ever more confusing and chaotic in proportion to your guests' level of alcohol consumption.

```
PROPS: NONE
IDEAL FOR HOUSE PARTIES          ★★★★★★+
AND LATE-NIGHT DRINKING SOIRÉES
```

Example game:
* Player 1 – 'Nicole Kidman'
* Player 2 – 'Kevin Spacey'
* Player 3 – 'Slim Shady'
        (change of direction)
* Player 4 – 'Ben Stiller'
* Player 5 – 'Cate Blanchett'
* Player 6 – 'Sofia Coppola'
* Player 7 – 'Sharon Stone'
        (change of direction)

How to play

The basic format for the game is the classic scenario of players sitting round a table or in a circle, with the turn rotating round each of the guests.

Each player must name a famous person (you can use specific types of celebrity if you want to restrict the game's scope) and you can start the game yourself by naming anyone you like. The next player, however, must follow with a star whose first name begins with the initial letter of the surname of the player you named. So, for example, if you had said Nicole Kidman, the second player could say Kevin Spacey. Player 3 would then have to say the name of person whose first name begins with 'S'.

The game carries on in this fashion until a player announces somebody whose first and last names start with the same letter – such as Mickey Mouse, Gareth Gates, Slim Shady, Michael Moore. The game's pattern is reversed; so, players must now follow with names where the subject's second name starts with the same letter as the previous celebrity's first name (see box). A change of direction also occurs when a named celeb has only one name, such as Sting or Dido.

Anybody who messes up or hesitates loses and everyone plays on an elimination basis until only one person is left – the winner.

The gentleman prefers...

A risqué and highly amusing verbal game that is not for the easily offended. Embarrassment is guaranteed as your guests push the boundaries of decency to new limits.

PROPS: NONE
IDEAL FOR SINGLES' PARTIES ★★★★★

How to play

This game can be played around the dinner table or with guests seated on the floor. Start the game yourself by announcing: 'The gentleman prefers...'

The turn now moves in a clockwise direction, with each player naming something that the gentleman prefers, for example:

* 'to be dominated'
* 'gimp masks to hair nets'
* 'pert butts'

Each player must repeat the original statement and all the suggestions that have gone before and then add another. So, the fourth player in our example would say: 'The gentleman prefers to be dominated, gimp masks to hair nets, pert butts and (additionally) pedigree animals.'

As the game progresses the suggestions become more lewd and the sensitive start to blush. If a player messes up or is unable to add to the list of preferences, he must perform a forfeit (see page 126) or take a drinking penalty, which will hopefully lessen his inhibitions and loosen his tongue for when his next turn arrives.

Continue playing until you run out of ideas or the list becomes impossible to remember.

Talking nonsense

An uncomplicated game that requires no props, just a little imagination, clicking fingers, large quantities of alcohol and a sense of humour.

```
PROPS: NONE                    ★★★★★★+
IDEAL FOR NOISY HOUSE PARTIES
```

How to play

Players should sit round a table or in a circle in the middle of the room. Begin by getting everybody to click their fingers in a consistent rhythm. Once a good rhythm has been established, the first player starts the game off by saying a word at random. The next player must say a word that either rhymes with the first word or begins with the same letter, and so on.

For example:
'duck', click, click, click...
'luck', click, click, click...
'lick', click, click, click...
'loose', click, click, click...
'goose', click, click, click...
and so on.

It sounds simple enough, but what you'll find is that once a rhythm has been established people try to maintain the sense of harmony by rhyming, rather than going for the simpler option of choosing a word with the same starting letter. The results can be nonsensical and, at times, offensive. At some point you are guaranteed to find one of your guests sitting wide-mouthed with a blank expression as she struggles to think of a rhyming word.

Any player who messes up has to face a forfeit (see page 126).

Variations

* Increase the pressure on players by demanding that they respond inside a set number of clicks (usually three)
* Insist on rhyming only
* Assign drinking penalties instead of forfeits

Cool-cat, idol or legend

A simple game that plays on nothing more than the childish (but eternally amusing) practice of making your friends suggest that they are attracted to people of the same sex.

PROPS: NONE
IDEAL FOR DRUNKEN EVENINGS
IN BARS AND CLUBS

★★★★★★+

How to play

As host and game organizer your job is to act as game caller and drink supplier. However, before the game begins you must explain clearly to the players how the game works. Tell them that, when the game begins, you will point at them randomly and say either:

* ★ 'cool-cat'
* ★ 'idol'
* ★ 'legend'

If you say 'cool-cat' they must give the name of a celebrity of the same sex whom they think is cool (George Clooney, Robbie Williams or Michael Jordan are the kind of names you'd expect boys to come out with here). If you say 'legend' they must name a person they admire or respect (my mum, Nelson Mandela or Bono are the type of answers you could expect here). Finally, if you say 'idol' they must name somebody that they fancy (no need for further explanation).

Players must reply immediately, without erring or hesitating. If they commit any of these offences or if they give an obviously wrong answer (saying the Pope when asked to a name an idol, for example) they must face a forfeit (see page 126).

The organ grinder

No props required, just five simple questions and you've all you need to drink, laugh and call your close friends 'monkeys'.

PROPS: NONE
IDEAL FOR PARTIES ROUND
THE TABLE AND LATE-NIGHT DRINKING

★★★★★★★★+

How to play

It is best to seat your players round a table for this game. The basic premise is that you ask each player five questions (see box), but the player in question (hereafter known as the 'monkey') says nothing and lets her 'organ grinder' (the player to her right) answer for her. Questions can be answered honestly but it is more amusing if players give facetious answers.

If the 'monkey' speaks, smirks or laughs out loud, the group shout 'he wasn't talking to the monkey, he was talking to the organ grinder!'; when this happens the 'monkey' performs a forfeit or takes a drink and the turn moves on to the next player.

Suggested questions and possible 'organ grinder' answers:

Q: 'What's your name, monkey?'

A: *The 'organ grinder' answers 'Norma' (even if her name is not Norma)*

Q: 'Are you a friendly monkey?'

A: *'Yes, she loves humans; no, she's got distemper'*

Q: 'How did you get here, monkey?'

A: *'She came in the car; she was trapped by bandits and abducted from the jungle'*

Q: 'Have you got a boyfriend, monkey?'

A: *'No, she's gay; yes, but she'd still like your phone number'*

Q: 'Do you miss your mother, monkey?'

A: *'Yes, she's picking her up in half an hour; no, she was snatched from her at birth'*

The adverb game

There's no doubt about it, there's nothing more satisfying than seeing your friends act like idiots. The adverb game gives you this precious opportunity. Like all the best games it's childish and there's no better way to get your party swinging than to get your super-tall, muscle-bound house-mate, dancing around the room on tip-toes.

PROPS: PAPER, PENS
IDEAL FOR DINNER PARTIES
OR GET-TOGETHERS WITH FRIENDS ★★★★+

Suggested adverbs:
* Brutally
* Camply
* Cruelly
* Energetically
* Flirtatiously
* Guiltily
* Lecherously
* Submissively
* Suggestively
* Teasingly

How to play

A nominated player writes down an adverb and passes it to Player 1. She then must act in the manner of the word that she's been given.

The other players then get to give instructions to the 'actor', all of which must be carried out in the manner of the adverb, for example 'sensually'. They may call out to her: 'undo your shirt', 'break dance' or 'kiss your hand' and she will have to attempt to do these in a 'sensual' manner.

The object of the game is to guess the word on the slip of paper.

The more risqué the adverbs and action, the more fun the game!

Who have you brought back?

A drunken and irreverent charades derivative that is sure to lead to more lewdness and hilarity than serious mime.

> PROPS: SCENARIO CARDS ★★★★★★★+
> (SEE BOX)
> IDEAL FOR LATE-NIGHT PARTIES

How to play

This is definitely a game best played in teams, with boys against girls. In classic charades' style, players mime to their team-mates who have 90 seconds to guess the scenario on the card that they are trying to portray. The twist is that the common theme to all the scenarios is that the 'mimer' has brought back somebody to his flat and has been engaged in some bizarre activity or another. The team must guess who the mystery visitor is and what they've been up to. The team with most points after a set number of rounds (or until everybody has had a turn) is declared the winner.

Suggested scenarios:

* Ben's mum... who came back for a thai massage
* Ben's grandma... who came back for an arm wrestling contest
* The girl next door... who came back to talk about her relationship problems
* A Russian waiter... who came back for late-night vodka slamming
* A Swedish au pair... who came back to explain about the benefits of saunas
* Ben's great granddad... who came round for a game of Twister

(The most obvious and lurid scenarios are not suitable for this publication.)

Sit-com challenge

A straightforward game that will test your guests' knowledge of popular culture. Those 'in the know' will get the chance to make their rivals squirm, while less-informed souls will suffer the indignity of forfeits or drinking penalties.

PROPS: NONE
IDEAL FOR ANY
ROUND-THE-TABLE PARTY ★★★★★+

How to play

Each guest, in turn, gets the chance to select the theme for a round of this game, but it's a good idea if you pick the theme for the first round to get the game up and running. Choose a TV show that is well known and which has a sizeable cast. The next player in the circle must now say the name of a character from the show, so if you had said ER (as the theme) the player to your left might have said 'Dr Carter'. The turn rotates round in a clockwise direction, with each player naming a different character from the show in question.

When the game stalls and a player is unable to think of a character from the show it's time for the punishments to begin. The player with whom the game stalled must either take a drinking penalty or face a forfeit (see page 126). In addition, the player who was last able to successfully name a character is free to select any other guest to make a confession to the group. As usual, if the confession is lame the group howls and groans and then imposes a forfeit or a drinking penalty.

Variations

If TV shows are not your thing, you can adapt the game to use alternative themes, for example:
* Sexual positions
* Exotic foods
* Footballers from particular teams or eras
* Music DJs
* Cocktails

The great outdoors

5

On warm sunny days what could be better than larking about outside with some pals? Whether you're a water fiend, love physical contact or prefer competitive eating games, you'll find something here that fits the bill.

Water bomb fend-off

This refreshing summer party classic is guaranteed to lead to you and your guests getting a thorough soaking.

> **PROPS: A DUSTBIN LID,** ★★★★★★★★★★+
> **WATER BOMBS (LOTS),**
> **TWO BUCKETS, ROPE (TO MARK OUT A CIRCLE),**
> **A MEASURING JUG, SPONGES**
> **IDEAL FOR SUNNY DAYS, POOL PARTIES**
> **AND BARBECUES**

What to do beforehand

Put an empty bucket in the middle of the garden and lay a rope around it with a radius of about 1.8 m (6 ft). Mark out a throwing line, behind which the players will have to stand, at the other end of the garden but within range.

How to play

Divide the group into male and female teams, and flick a coin to determine who goes first. The team captain stands behind the throwing line with his team and is given a bucket full of water bombs. You then take up position in the centre of the target rope. The players have 1 minute to get as many water bombs as possible into the target bucket and it's your job to try to deflect the bombs using the dustbin lid. At the end of the minute the contents of the target bucket is emptied into a measuring jug (after any unbroken water bombs are opened and poured into the bucket) and the volume of liquid is recorded.

The other team now has 1 minute to get more water into the bucket than their rivals. The losing team's punishment is to stand in the target circle and take a 30-second dousing with wet sponges from their rivals.

Apple bobbing

The original and still the best game for a Halloween party; what could be better than placing your face in a bucket of ice-cold water while blindfolded in order to bite on an old, pappy Granny Smith apple?

PROPS: APPLES, A LARGE BOWL OF WATER, BLINDFOLDS, A LARGE BOWL OF FLOUR (OPTIONAL), MARSHMALLOWS (OPTIONAL), BEER (OPTIONAL) ★★★★+
IDEAL FOR FESTIVE PARTIES AND OUTDOOR EVENTS

How to play

The game works best with a large bowl full of water that offers sufficient space for players to compete at the same time. Put two apples in the water and blindfold the players. On your command they dip their faces in the water and try to fish out an apple with their mouths; no hands allowed! The first to do so wins.

Getting messy

If you want to have a bit of extra fun, add on an extra 'bob'. Use a large bowl of flour with some marshmallows dotted around and after the apple bobbing is over get the players to dip for the sweet stuff instead. You can just imagine the results. Now, things are going to get really messy.

Who's for the beer bob?

Another version sees the apples replaced with small soft drinks bottles (500 ml; 17 floz), which are filled with beer. The players fish out the bottles with their mouths but once they're out they can use their hands to undo the lids and down the contents. The first to put an empty bottle on the table wins.

Competitive balloon pop

A simple game that will ensure your party descends into instant chaos; so, blow up those balloons and invite the neighbours over before they call the cops.

PROPS: BALLOONS, STRING
★★★★★★★★★★+
IDEAL FOR DRINKING PARTIES IN THE PARK

How to play

You'll need two teams for this game: boys and girls is the simplest split, with equal numbers of each. If dividing the players by gender doesn't work at your party, you'll have to use different coloured balloons for each team.

Each player ties a balloon securely to his left ankle. The players step forward into the playing area (a park or garden is best) and on your signal the game commences. The players must try to burst their rivals balloons while at the same time fending off attacks from their opponents. The task is made harder by the fact that players keep their arms behind their backs (tie them if there are any devious types who might cheat).

When a player's own balloon is popped he is out of the game. Play continues for a set time (2 minutes is ideal) or until one team has burst all of its opponent's balloons. When the dust settles, the team with the most players left is pronounced the winner.

Adding to the challenge

If the game proves too easy why not add blindfolds into the mix? But, be warned, it may lead to more bruising than some of your guests can tolerate.

Duelling (water) pistols

It wouldn't be a summer party without a water fight. So, don't disappoint your guests, indulge them in some watery fun and wait for the chaos to unfold before your eyes.

PROPS: TWO WATER PISTOLS, CANDLES
★★★★+
IDEAL FOR BARBECUES AND OUTDOOR PARTIES

What to do beforehand

You'll need two identical water pistols. Test them both before play begins and check their range. Place two candles on tables in the garden, spacing them well apart but within the range of the pistols.

How to play

Divide the players into two even teams (boys against girls is guaranteed to make the game more competitive) and place each team behind one of the candles. One player from each team steps forward and the candles are lit.

The two players stand back-to-back and then, at the host's signal, turn and start firing. The objective is to put out the opponent's candle before he can extinguish yours. The successful player earns a point for his team.

The game continues until every pair has completed their duel. The team with the most points is pronounced champion. Their prize is a complete drenching of their opponents, who must stand in a line in front of their candle. Warning: a full-scale water fight is likely to ensue.

Bend over

This game will appeal to the more supple and sober members of your party. Frequently this isn't the men – watch in amusement as they topple over one by one!

**PROPS: EMPTY CEREAL PACKET ★★★★★★★★+
IDEAL FOR BARBECUES AND
OUTDOOR PARTIES**

What to do beforehand

You'll need to find a cardboard cereal box, and tear off the flaps on the top. Make sure you take the cereal out first. Now place the box on the ground in a suitably grassy area – people are likely to end up in a heap on the floor so anything to soften the blow will be much appreciated. Now let the fun begin!

How to play

Members of the party take turns in bending over to pick up the box with their teeth. Sounds simple enough, but here's the catch – they must pick up the box using their teeth and only their feet can touch the floor. The first round should be pretty easy.

Now tear off an inch of card from the top of the box and let everyone try again. The most unsupple of the group will probably fall over during this round. Flexible friends will surprise you with how low they can go. The glory goes to the last player able to pick the box up, frequently just an inch-high box.

Your friends will be falling over themselves trying to win!

Ping-pong tumblers

A straightforward throwing game that brings all the fun of the fairground to your party without the heady odour of engine oil mixed with candyfloss.

PROPS: PING-PONG BALLS, TUMBLERS (TWO FOR EACH GUEST), A BOWL OF WATER, STRIPS OF PAPER, A PEN ★★★★+
IDEAL FOR HOUSE PARTIES AND BARBECUES

How to play

Gather up your players and seat them around a table. The bowl of water is positioned in the middle of the table, with the tumblers (which are half-filled with water) circling it. Write the names of the players on separate strips of paper and put one under each glass; or, if you can't find a pen and paper, position the glasses in a way that corresponds with the guests' seating positions.

The first player is given the ping-pong ball and, from a seated position, she must try to throw it into one of the tumblers. If the throw is successful, the player whose name is underneath must perform a forfeit (see page 126). However, if her throw rebounds into the bowl of water, she must face a forfeit herself.

Variation

If you want to play this one as a drinking game then you'll need two tumblers and one shot glass per player as well as the bowl of water. This time for successful throws the person whose name is underneath the glass has to drink a shot. But if the player fails to get the ball into a tumbler, she has to drink the shot instead. You could also add an 'all players drink' when the ball is deflected into the bowl rather than just the inaccurate marksman responsible.

Pass the key

This is undoubtedly an outdoor party game that is best played after your guests have had a few drinks. When the players' fine motor skills are fading and their balance is not all it should be, falling over is then pretty much guaranteed.

PROPS: FOUR VERY COLD KEYS, ★★★★★★★★+
TWO LENGTHS OF STRING
IDEAL FOR LARGE OUTDOOR PARTIES

How to play

If you have a large number of guests this game is best played outside. Divide the group into two teams – mixed groups of male and female players are the most embarrassing and therefore the most amusing.

Give each team a length of string with a key tied at each end. For maximum impact you can put the keys in a deep freeze for a couple of hours before the party so that they are suitably cold to the touch.

The players in each team stand in a line shoulder to shoulder and the keys are passed up and down trouser legs, skirts, tops and dresses from one end of the line to the other. The players are allowed to help one another but their efforts should only add to the general embarrassment.

The first team to successfully pass the keys from one end of the line to the other is the winner. The losing team should be made to pay a team forfeit (see page 126).

Hula contest

There's nothing like a little childish behaviour to get your summer party swinging, so swivel those hips and get your hulas hooping and your guests whooping.

PROPS: HULA HOOPS, A PADDLING POOL FULL OF COLD WATER
IDEAL FOR SUMMER PARTIES AND OUTDOOR EVENTS ★★★★★★+

How to play

The rules are straightforward: each guest must swing a hula hoop for a set time; if they don't, they have to take a dip in a paddling pool freshly filled with cold water. The hardest part for you – the game's leader – is to determine the time limit for a successful hula hoop. For complete novices 1 minute will seem an eternity but experts (usually girls with snake-like hips) will be able to hula their hoops for what seems like days on end. Thirty seconds for men and one minute for women is probably a good starting point.

Variations

* If you would rather play the game for prizes rather than the forfeit of a dip in the pool, you can time each player and reward the most accomplished.
* If one hula hoop is not enough of a challenge try using multiple hoops and give a prize to the player who can hula for a minute with the most hoops.

Doughnut variety pack

If ever there was a comedy food it's the humble doughnut. So, if you're having a party get some in. They're round, they're tasty and they've got a hole in the middle. The perfect party foodstuff.

PROPS: DOUGHNUTS, COCKTAIL STICKS, STRING, TWO BOWLS, BOWLS OF WATER, BLINDFOLDS
IDEAL FOR GARDEN PARTIES AND BARBECUES

★★★★★+

How to play

You may want to do one, two or all three of these fun foodie games. Each successfully retrieved doughnut represents a team point.

Round 1 – Blindfolded doughnut eating

Divide the players into two teams. One player from each team steps forward, dons a blindfold and awaits a signal from the game organizer (that's you). At the other end of the garden two doughnuts are put in bowls next to four identical bowls filled with water. The bowls are mixed around so nobody knows which is which. At the starter's signal the two players creep forward until they find the table. Their objective is to find and eat a doughnut before their rival.

Round 2 – Pass the doughnut

Players are once more divided into two teams, which are lined up shoulder to shoulder. Each player is given a cocktail stick to hold in their mouth, and the player at the end of each line is given a ring doughnut. The doughnut is skewered onto the cocktail stick and on the starter's signal the game commences. The players must try to move the doughnut from one end of the line to the other using only their cocktail sticks. If the doughnut is dropped it must go back to the beginning and the process begun again.

Round 3 – Eat the doughnut from the tree

This game is played in a similar fashion to Round 1, the only difference is that this time the blindfolded players must reach and eat a doughnut suspended from a tree branch via a string.

Going down with your ship

Pouring water into bowls doesn't sound like something that could inspire either great hilarity or drunkenness, but – surprisingly – it can. Going down with your ship is a game with all the addictive qualities of Jenga but without the wooden blocks and grandma cheating.

PROPS: TWO BOWLS (ONE SMALLER THAN THE OTHER), A TUMBLER FOR EACH PLAYER, A SHOT GLASS FOR EACH PLAYER, WATER, PLENTY TO DRINK
IDEAL FOR BARBECUES, GARDEN PARTIES AND AFTER-DINNER DRINKING

★★★★★+

How to play

Fill a washing-up bowl two-thirds with water and float a smaller bowl on its surface. Each player is given a tumbler full of water and an empty shot glass.

Start the game yourself, emptying some of the water from your tumbler into the floating bowl. The turn now moves to the player on your left and continues around the group in a clockwise direction, with each player pouring a little more water into the bowl.

The game continues in this way until one player's contribution makes the bowl sink. The offending player must either take a forfeit (see page 126) or have his shot glass filled and must drink. The bowl is emptied, put back on the surface of the water and the game resumes. Continue until your fine motor skills desert you.

103

Garden jousting

A mindless and childish game that is as funny as it is futile. Four players, four wooden spoons and a competitive spirit are all you'll need for this variant on piggy-back fighting.

> **PROPS: FOUR WOODEN SPOONS ★★★★+
> (OR PLASTIC SERVING SPOONS),
> ORANGES OR POTATOES
> IDEAL FOR SUMMER PARTIES IN PARKS AND GARDENS**

How to play

Divide your group into two teams of equal numbers and give each a pair of wooden spoons and an orange or smallish potato. Two players from each team contest each round of the game; with one player in each combination acting as horse and the other as knight.

You can play the game in piggy-back riding style, with the knight hitching a ride on the horse's shoulders or you can have the horse crawl around on his hands and knees. Whichever option you choose, the objective of the game remains the same.

The knight balances the fruit (or veg) on one of the spoons, which is held out in front of him. The second spoon is held in the other hand and used as a weapon. When both pairs are ready the action begins. The two knights ride out to meet each other with spoons flailing and try to knock the other's orange (or potato) on to the floor. The first team to do so wins the opening round.

Fruity croquet

As the English aristocracy know only too well, a summer party is not complete without a game of croquet. Of course, the traditional game with its manicured lawns and wooden mallets is not very now. So why not try this 21st-century version where you shove some fruit down your tights, wiggle your hips and rise to the challenge of all new Fruity Croquet.

> **PROPS: FRUIT, STOCKINGS, BELTS, START AND FINISH LINES IDEAL FOR OUTDOOR PARTIES** ★★★★★★+

How to play

You can play this game in teams (women against men is, of course, best) or you can play winner-stays-on in a head-to-head knockout format. Whichever you choose, the gameplay is the same.

Put three pieces of round, firm fruit (apples and oranges are ideal) into a stocking leg (tights or pantyhose work equally well) and tie a knot to keep the three fruits packed down at the bottom of the hose. Tie the other end to the centre of the player's belt so that the stocking dangles toward the ground between her legs – this is the improvised croquet mallet.

Both players must be equipped in this way before the game can start. Set up a start line and then about 6 m (20 ft) away set a finish line.

The two players step forward to the start line where they address the ball (a tennis ball or another apple or orange). Upon your signal the players race to hit the ball, from the start to finish line, using only their 'croquet mallets'; they have to wiggle their hips and perform all manner of dance moves to control the dangling fruit and hit the ball.

This would be a perfect moment to capture on video – so make sure you're ready to start filming.

From ladle to mouth

It's not clever and it's not sophisticated, but eating mashed potato with an egg whisk is undeniably funny, especially if the player alongside is attempting the same feat with a fish slice!

> **PROPS: KITCHEN UTENSILS, TRAY, BOWLS, MASHED POTATO OR RICE PUDDING**
> **IDEAL FOR OUTDOOR PARTIES**
> ★★★★+

Suggested foodstuffs and utensils:

✳ Mashed potato	✳ Whisk
✳ Rice pudding	✳ Chopsticks
✳ Peas	✳ Spatula
✳ Jelly	✳ Fish slice
✳ Ice-cream	✳ Rolling pin
✳ Tripe	✳ Potato masher

How to play

Place an assortment of kitchen utensils (see box) on a tray. Get all the players to select an item but do not tell them what they will have to do with it.

Seat the players and put a bowl of mashed potato or rice pudding in front of each of them (you could also try other types of food – see box). On your command they start eating, using only the implement they have chosen. The first player to clear her bowl is the winner... or if you can't wait that long, give them a time limit (2 minutes is plenty) and see who's eaten the most at the end of the round.

Variation

If you want to make the task a little harder you can insist on the players wearing blindfolds, using their weaker hand or just their little fingers. You can also introduce penalties if food falls on to the floor.

Marshmallow eat-off

A messy eating game that is best played outside. But beware, nausea can be a problem for those whose stomachs object to too much of the sugary sweet marshmallows.

PROPS: TWO BOWLS, ICING SUGAR, ★★★★★★+
LOTS OF MARSHMALLOWS
IDEAL FOR POOL PARTIES AND BARBECUES

How to play

Play this game as a head-to-head. Pair up the players (try to match them in terms of age, athletic ability and gluttony) and line them up in front of two bowls.

Place ten marshmallows (the classic pink and white ones are best) in a bowl full of icing sugar, mix the sugary concoction around and stand back. You will, of course, need both bowls stocked in this way. On your command the two players come forward, place their hands behind their backs and stick their faces in the icing sugar. The first to finish is the winner and the loser faces a forfeit (see page 126).

Eat the pinks version

Put five pink and five white marshmallows in the bowl and place an identical empty bowl next to it on the table. The players must eat the pinks and decant the whites from the icing sugar into the empty bowl. Any mistakes are punished by an instant forfeit and the bowl is restocked. The player who finishes the task first is the winner. The loser has to perform a forfeit.

Blowing bubbles

If you like food and drink and don't mind getting downright messy then this is the game for you. If you prefer to keep clean, bibs or protective clothing are highly recommended.

> PROPS: BUBBLEGUM,
> FRUIT CHEWS, PAPER PLATES,
> WHIPPED CREAM, BLINDFOLDS, BIBS
> IDEAL FOR OUTDOOR PARTIES AND AS
> A PRECURSOR TO FOOD FIGHTS
>
> ★★★★★

What to do beforehand

Place a piece of bubblegum on a paper plate with a few chewy fruit gums (which act as decoys) and cover the whole ensemble in aerosol spray cream. If you want to make the game harder you can leave the wrappers on the confectionery. You'll need two plates furnished in this way.

How to play

The players are divided into two teams and one player from each steps up to contest the first round. The players are blindfolded and sat in front of their plates. On your signal they must put their faces in the creamy mess and fish out the gum. The first player to get the gum, open the wrapper and then blow a bubble wins. You can play for points or to avoid penalties.

If you want to continue the food-based fun you can add in additional rounds:

* Cracker eating – once the player has successfully blown a bubble, he moves on to a second plate filled with dried crackers. The players must consume the dry biscuits and then whistle a tune.
* Water belching – to complete the game players must down a pint of water without pausing, then belch. The first to do so wins the game.

'Did I say that?'

6

Did you know that one of your closest friends has had a crush on your sister? Or that your ex-lover had a same-sex romantic encounter? Unlock sordid secrets and confess a few of your own with these games that make people say things that they might regret in the morning.

Spin the bottle

An all-time party classic that should not be ignored simply because you've been playing it since the age of 12.

> **PROPS: AN EMPTY BOTTLE TO SPIN, DRINK (OPTIONAL) IDEAL FOR ALL PARTIES**   ★★★★★★★+

How to play

Few people in the English-speaking world can have reached the age of consent without ever having played Spin the Bottle. But, just in case you are one of that curious minority, the basic game works as follows: the guests are seated on the floor in a circle and an empty bottle (glass ones work best) is handed to the first player.

The player spins the bottle and when it comes to a halt the player at whom it is pointing must take centre stage.

There are several variations here:

* Kissing – the spinner has to kiss the player the bottle points to
* Making a confession
* Doing a forfeit (see page 126)
* Drinking penalties – for this version, you will need either a large variety of bottled drinks (beers, wines or spirits) or glasses filled with alcohol. Set the drinks out in a circle, scattering a few glasses of water to offer hope to the already inebriated, and put the bottle in the middle. The players spin the bottle in turn and whatever beverage it finishes up pointing to is the one the spinner must drink

Tell it like it is

simple game with great potential for embarrassment and drunkenness – which makes it the perfect game for any late-night gathering.

PROPS: NONE
IDEAL FOR LATE-NIGHT
DRINKING SESSIONS

★★★★+

How to play

The game begins with the players placing their hands on top of each others' on a table. Each player first puts down their right hand, another player puts down their hand on top of it, the players continue until they have each put down both hands.

The player whose hand went down first then calls out a number, for example four. The players then remove their hands from the top of the heap, one by one, until they reach the fourth hand from the bottom. The host asks the player whose hand was fourth a question (see box). She must answer the question honestly; if the other players (who act as judge and jury) decide that the answer is dishonest, she must offer up a confession. If she is judged to have answered honestly, her prize is

Suggested questions:

* Are you attracted to anybody at the party?
* Do you dislike anybody at the party?
* Have you ever kissed any of the party guests?
* Have you been drunk (apart from tonight) in the last week?
* Have you ever left a restaurant without paying your bill?
* Are you intending to seduce anyone tonight?
* Can you keep a secret? If so, what's the longest you ever kept one without telling a soul?
* What colour is your underwear?
* Have you ever lied to a partner?

that she calls out a new number and poses the next question once all the players have reassembled their hands.

Naughty numbers

Eyes down for this naughty number matching game that will lead to revelations about the rest of your partygoers.

> **PROPS: CARDS, PENS**
> **IDEAL FOR LATE-NIGHT GATHERINGS** ★★★★+

What to do beforehand

You will need a card and a pen for each player. Draw a simple grid on each of the cards with six random numbers (from 1 to 20) on them. Try to vary the numbers on the cards so that each card is unique.

How to play

The party host acts as caller and asks questions randomly (rather than in sequence) from the numbered list (see box). State the number of the question clearly before reading it out.

The players cross out the corresponding number on their card if they can answer 'yes' to the question. So, for example, if the question was, '4, Have you ever cheated on a boyfriend or girlfriend?' any guests who are guilty of such romantic duplicity must put a cross over the number 4 on their card.

The first player to cross out all six numbers is the winner and officially the party's biggest hedonist. Keep playing until only one player is left. The losing player has either been dishonest or has lived such a straight life that they deserve to take a forfeit (see page 126); or, if you prefer, make a confession.

Twenty questions:

1 Have you ever been in a band?
2 Have you ever had a one-night stand?
3 Have you ever stolen anything from a shop?
4 Have you ever cheated on a boyfriend or girlfriend?
5 Have you consumed an illegal substance?
6 Have you been to a doctor with an embarrassing ailment?
7 Have you had a holiday romance?
8 Have you kissed somebody whose name you don't know in the last six months?
9 Have you been intimate with any other guests at the party?
10 Have you indulged in karaoke in the last year?
11 Have you been to a party uninvited in the last year?
12 Have you lied about your age or job to impress a member of the opposite sex?
13 Have you ever taken a camera or video camera into the bedroom?
14 Have you had a fist fight or cat fight as an adult?
15 Have you ignored a mobile phone call from a girlfriend or boyfriend in the last month?
16 Have you ever been intimate with a member of the same sex?
17 Have you ever been asked to leave a bar or nightclub?
18 Have you got a tattoo?
19 Have you ever been interrupted during sex?
20 Have you taken a day off work for a hangover in the last month?

Bluffer's confessions

This variation of Truth or Dare is guaranteed to get your party rocking and raucous. It's basically a confessional game, with a little bluff thrown in. Best of all, it's a game that develops gradually from a sedate start to become as controversial as you like. Be warned, you may live to regret your honesty!

> **PROPS: PENS, SLIPS OF PAPER**
> **IDEAL FOR DINNER PARTIES**
> **OR GET-TOGETHERS WITH FRIENDS** ★★★★+

How to play

To begin, place all fragile egos and inhibitions in a safe place. Gather your players around a table and give each a pen and some slips of paper. Then, elect a chairperson. One player starts by writing down three 'acts' on separate slips of paper. Two 'acts' should be bluffs, while one must be something that the player has actually done.

For example, she could write:

* I once put salt instead of sugar in my boss's coffee
* I once helped myself to money from the petty cash tin at work
* I once went to work drunk

One act is true, whereas the others are red herrings. The slips of paper are passed to the game's chairperson who reads them out.

It is now the job of the remaining players to guess which of the 'acts' is true. After a brief conference (set a time limit of 1 minute), the group must make their decision. If they guess correctly, the player loses and has to take a forfeit (see page 126).

To get people in the swing of things, it's a good idea to start by restricting the confessions to fairly safe areas, for example work or school. Once they get into the game, you can make categories more personal.

Your number's up!

The key to any good game is simplicity; if it's too complicated you won't play it. Thankfully, this game is as straightforward as they come. It's basically Truth or Dare but with dice.

> PROPS: THREE DICE,
> FORFEIT CARDS ★★★★★+
> IDEAL FOR ANY ROUND-THE-TABLE PARTY

What to do beforehand

Prior to the game, you will need to write out your dare cards (six in all, each containing six numbered forfeits); get some ideas from the box right or see page 126. Put the cards in a safe place with your three dice and wait for a a good moment to start off the game.

How to play

Keep back one of the dice for forfeits. The first player rolls the remaining two dice, announces her score and hands them to the next player. Player 2 must then decide if she will roll a 'higher' or 'lower' number than the first player. Once she has made her prediction, the dice are rolled. If the prediction is right, the dice move on to the next player; but if it is wrong, she has to ask 'Truth or dare?'.

> Suggested 'dares':
> * Balance a bottle of beer on your head and walk from one end of the room to the other
> * Have an ice cube placed in your belly button and keep it there until it melts
> * Drink a tablespoon of tabasco or chilli sauce
> * Without using any hands, lap up a saucer of milk

If the group opts for 'dare', she must roll the forfeit dice twice. The first roll selects the dare card and the second picks the numbered dare. She must fulfil the dare to the satisfaction of the other players, otherwise she must take a drink as well.

If the group selects 'truth' then she must make a confession.

Bluffer's delight

This simple bluffing game can be played at the start of a party to help break the ice or later on in the evening for drinking penalties.

PROPS: A COIN, A CUP OR HAT **★★★★★★+**
IDEAL FOR LATE-NIGHT
DRINKING PARTIES

Suggested themes:
* Schooldays
* The workplace
* Romantic situations
* Family business
* The sports field
* Childhood
* Holidays
* Celebrity connections
* Disco dancing

How to play

This game works best if you restrict the players to particular themes (see box) for their stories. Sit the players around a table and give one of them a coin and the cup (or hat). Explain to the players that when it is their turn they will have 10 seconds to gather their thoughts and decide whether they are going to tell a truthful story or a bluff. If it is a bluff, the player discreetly places the coin tails up under the cup; if it is based on truth, he places the coin heads up.

The player tells his story and the rest of the group must try to guess if it was an honest anecdote or a completely fabricated one. When they have decided they say 'truth' or 'bluff' and the player turns over the cup to reveal whether they are correct or not.

If the group is right, the player must make a confession or take a forfeit (see page 126). If they are wrong, everyone else in the group must confess or perform a forfeit.

Toilet paper confessions

There are many complex routes you can take to get your guests to make confessions, but none can match the ease of getting them to tear up toilet paper as a precursor to invading their personal lives.

PROPS: A TOILET ROLL
IDEAL FOR RAUCOUS
LATE-NIGHT PARTIES   ★★★★★+

How to play

Assemble your guests but don't tell them what game you're about to play. When everybody is ready, pass a toilet roll to the first player in the circle. Tell them that they must remove some paper from the roll and that it's up to them how many sheets they tear off. Once they've torn off what they want, they pass it on to the next player, who does likewise.

The roll travels round the circle, with you reminding everybody that they can tear off as much or as little as they like. With any luck some of your more boisterous guests will end up with huge bundles of triple-ply; thankfully, the smug satisfaction they've gained from their hysterical high jinks will soon disappear.

Once everybody is sitting holding their lavatory paper you can then explain to them how the game works. Each player must now make one confession for each sheet of paper they hold. Watch jaws drop as the greedy loo-roll grabbers now have to contemplate the challenge that faces them.

Go round the group and listen to the confessions; but if the group believes a revelation is either too tame or unbelievable they can rule that the offending player must do a forfeit or take a drink penalty.

'I have never...'

Players admit their vices, misdemeanours and indiscretions without going into graphic detail or naming names (unless they want to). It's a great way to get an evening of games underway. Alcohol isn't essential, but booze will certainly help loosen a few tongues.

```
PROPS: NONE                      ★★★★+
IDEAL FOR POST-DINNER
PARTY HILARITY
```

How to play

Gather your friends together and sit everybody in a circle. Ideally, you should try to choose close friends or people who tend to share secrets, in that way they are more likely to tell the truth.

One player (usually you) begins and makes a true statement, beginning with the phrase 'I have never...' (see box). For example, 'I have never been to a gym' then, if any other players haven't been to a gym either, they give a signal – this could be raising their hands or taking a swig of their drinks. Those that don't give the signal are conspicuous by their inaction and are invited to explain themselves.

Suggested statements:
Try these (but only if they're true!)
* 'I have never lied to my partner'
* 'I have never caused a traffic accident'
* 'I have never taken illegal substances'
* 'I have never peed in a swimming pool or a shower'
* 'I have never fancied any of you'
* 'I have never been arrested'

The game will often start tamely but the statements soon get more personal and revealing. But be warned, the game will only work if people are honest.

Q & A

If you want to test how much you really know about your friends, this is the game for you. Three questions, three answers and then you get your chance to use your powers of deduction. Guess right and keep your dignity... guess wrong and face a forfeit.

PROPS: SCRAPS OF PAPER, PENS
IDEAL FOR GROUPS
OF CLOSE FRIENDS

How to play

The first player (usually, the host) asks the group three questions. The group must resist the temptation to quip straight back and instead write down their answers on a piece of paper. The papers are then signed and collected up by a spokesperson.

The spokesperson reads the answers out and the player who posed the questions must try to guess, one by one, whose answers are whose.

Suggested questions:

* When was the last time you took a day off work because you were hungover?
* How many one night stands have you had?
* How many units of alcohol have you consumed so far this week?
* What's your most embarrassing moment as a child?
* What's your most embarrassing moment as an adult?
* Have you ever gone skinny dipping?
* What's your favourite music track of all time?
* When was the last time you did karaoke?

121

Truth or dare pass the parcel

A straightforward route (without any need for explaining complicated rules) to the kind of Truth or Dare gameplay that is guaranteed to cause laughs and blushes.

> **PROPS: A PARCEL WRAPPED UP** ★★★★★★+
> **WITH TRUTH AND DARE CARDS**
> **INSIDE ITS LAYERS, MUSIC**
> **IDEAL FOR MIXED GATHERINGS**

What to do beforehand

Like regular Pass the Parcel, the success of this game lies in the preparation. Build your parcel around something fairly rigid such as a shoe box. Wrap it up with plenty of newspaper and tape, inserting the Truth and Dare cards between the layers and – if you're feeling generous – you can always mix in a few sweets every now and then to give the 'unwrappers' hope that they might get a treat rather than a trial.

How to play

Little explanation is surely necessary here. First, you'll need a DJ to control the music. The players pass the parcel around the circle and when the music stops the player holding the parcel gets to unwrap a layer of paper. If there's nothing in there, the game continues; but if there's a Truth or Dare card beneath the paper then there's a brief pause while the unlucky player dishes the dirt or performs a forfeit (see page 126).

Dare cards

Try some of these or refer to the forfeits on page 126.

* Dance the Macarena while singing Baa-baa black sheep.
* Women only – remove your bra without taking your top off.
* Men only – put a bra on and keep it on for half an hour.

Truth cards

You can allow the player to make a confession of their own choosing but if you would rather control the proceedings write out personal questions for them to answer.

* Have you ever cheated on a boyfriend or girlfriend?
* Have you had a secret dalliance with any of the other players here?
* Have you got your eye on anybody at the party?
* Have you lied to any friends or family this week?
* Have you ever been in a police cell?

My wildest dream

A suggestive version of the classic 'Guess who?' format that is sure to push the boundaries of decency and plumb the depths of depravity... and all without leaving the dining table.

> PROPS: PENS, PAPER, STICKY MEMO NOTES
> ★★★★+
> IDEAL FOR ROUND-THE-TABLE PARTIES

How to play

There are two ways of playing this game:

Twenty questions

The players take it in turn to be the subject of a 20-questions' inquiry in this version. Prior to the inquisition, the subject writes down her wildest dream on a piece of paper, which is folded over and placed in an envelope. The group now has 20 questions with which to identify the subject's fantasy. As usual, the questions asked can only be met with a 'yes' or 'no' reply.

Guess who? style

In this variation, each player writes down details of a fantastical dream on a sticky memo note. When everybody is ready each player sticks their note onto the forehead of the player sitting to their left. The questioning now begins.

The turn moves round the group in a clockwise direction, starting with the party host. With each turn a player asks one question about the fantasy described on her forehead. The group collectively replies, but can only answer 'yes' or 'no'. If the answer to the question is 'yes', the player gets to pose another question. However, when the group answers 'no', the turn moves on to the next player. Players can guess at what is written on the sticky note at any time during their turn, but if they guess incorrectly their turn comes to an end.

The game continues until only one frustrated soul is left still struggling to identify the fantasy displayed on her forehead. Make the player in question face a forfeit (see page 126) for being so slow.

Who knows me best?

An amusing game that tests guests' knowledge of their host but which can also be adapted and applied to all the other party guests.

PROPS: A LIST OF TEN
QUESTIONS, PAPER, PENS,
A PRIZE (BOTTLE OF BUBBLY)
IDEAL FOR DINNER PARTIES AND SINGLES' NIGHTS

★★★★★+

What to do beforehand

Prior to the party you will need to write down a list of ten questions that will probe your guests' knowledge of you and your past. The more personal the questions the more amusing the answers, so don't be bashful (see box).

Record the correct answers on a piece of paper, which should be placed in an envelope on the table.

How to play

Give all the players a list of the questions, a pen and 1 minute to record their answers. Then, gather up the papers and quickly mark them. The player with the most correct answers is the winner and receives a prize. If the guests enjoy the game, you can adapt the questions, as necessary, and let each of them have a turn at being the subject.

Suggested questions:

* Who was my first love?
* Have I ever cheated on a girlfriend or boyfriend?
* What is my drink of choice?
* Have I ever been out in drag?
* Which party guests have I had a romantic encounter with?
* Have I ever had a holiday romance?
* At what age did I lose my virginity?
* Have I ever had a romantic encounter with a member of the same sex?
* Do I prefer blondes or brunettes?
* Have I ever wet myself laughing?

Forfeits

* Pole dance around a broom for one minute

* Sing a song from a musical in the style of Bon Jovi or Pavarotti

* Confess the last person you had a dirty dream about

* Kiss the feet of every player

* Impersonate your favourite superhero for the next 30 minutes

* Use only your nose to push a cork across the floor a set distance (hands must be behind your back)

* Sing a tender love song

* Perform a cartwheel, handstand or forward roll depending on your gymnastic abilities

* Spend a minute telling another player how much you love them

* Inhale helium from a balloon and sing the theme tune of your favourite soap opera

* Eat as much jelly as you can using a knife and fork

* Stand in the street and shout 'I'm a furry hamster!'

* Tell a joke in the style of Arnold Schwarzenegger

* Parade around the room in the style of a chicken

* Eat a doughnut without licking your lips

Team games

* Swap a piece of clothing with another member of the team (without leaving the room). The host can specify the item of clothing if they're feeling particularly vindictive

* Pay a compliment to each player in the opposing team

* Each player must give a member of the opposing team a 2-minute foot massage

* Players must allow make-up to be applied to their faces by the opposing team for 5 minutes

* Each player must dance with a team member of the same sex

Index

Acknowledgements

Executive Editor: Trevor Davies
Editor: Charlotte Wilson
Executive Art Editor: Rozelle Bentheim
Design: Grade Design Consultants, London
Illustrator: Yann
Production Controller: Ian Paton